FASHION

PORTFOLIO

A portfolio is the mirror of a designer. At a glance it showcases one's aesthetic, thinking process, ability to create and potential to execute.

Lubov Azria
Chief Creative Officer
BCBGMAXAZRIAGROUP

FASHION
PORTFOLIO

DESIGN AND PRESENTATION

ANNA KIPER

BATSFORD

Author Anna Kiper

First published in the United Kingdom in 2014 by
B.T. Batsford, 43 Great Ormond Street, London WC1N 3HZ

An Imprint of B.T. Batsford Holdings Ltd

Copyright © B.T. Batsford 2014
Text and images © Anna Kiper unless stated otherwise

ISBN 9781849940856

A CIP catalogue record for this book is available from the
British Library.

15 14 13 12 11 10 9

Reproduction by Dot Gradations Ltd, UK
Printed and bound by Leo Paper Products Ltd, China

This book can be ordered direct from the publisher at
www.batsford.com, or try your local bookshop.

FSC
www.fsc.org

MIX
Paper from
responsible sources
FSC® C020056

CONTENTS

INTRODUCTION

What is fashion — art or craft? The common perception is that fashion always has a practical, utilitarian purpose. However, on occasion, brilliant, creative minds elevate fashion to the level of art, affecting our minds and emotions with their vision, telling us powerful stories and transporting us to their imaginary worlds through their collections.

Fashion geniuses have transformed society by changing common perceptions — Chanel liberated women, giving them an independent, powerful look marked by a military-styled tweed suit; Dior brought back the hour-glass silhouette, instilling femininity into post-war fashion; Comme des Garçons questioned human form and shape, thereby redefining the traditional concept of female beauty through garment deconstruction and an all-black attire; and McQueen, with his unleashed, burning talent brought a strong emotional component to his collections, constantly referring to death and his personal struggles. Balenciaga and Ferré forever merged architecture and fashion, while Issey Miyake and Hussein Chalayan explored innovative ways to fuse fashion with technology. Miyake was fascinated by the technical process of garment creation, the inherent mishaps, and therefore the innovation that occurred throughout the stages. Chalayan broke away from the traditional materials of fashion, using pieces of plastic from cars and metal from airplanes.

Probably one of the most fascinating achievements in fashion was Elsa Schiaparelli's design approach. Rather than following the more traditional method of designing collections around individual looks inspired by the latest textiles and embellishments, she introduced the idea of storytelling through her collections, which were inspired by distinct and complex themes. Decades later, Yves Saint Laurent, fascinated by the narrative method, developed his Out-of-Africa safari story and Russian collection, tying together all elements such as textiles, silhouettes, styling, and mood to make a cohesive presentation. Designers today continue with this effective approach.

This book sheds light on the many ways a designer can pursue the creative process. Many designers surround themselves with beautiful objects, images and textiles to create an inspirational environment that sparks design ideas. Some gravitate to the technical language of draping and construction. Others emphasise sketching as the primary design tool, endlessly documenting their ideas on paper, and some, on the contrary, deconstruct and reconstruct vintage clothes, inspired by the transformation of the garment.

No matter what the creative approach is, it is critical to capture personal vision in the form of the design journal and portfolio. As designers evolve and mature, the fashion portfolio needs to express their current state of mind, design aesthetic, world perceptions and unique life experiences.

Designers have an important responsibility to society. They are the beauty and style receptacles, collecting and filtering cultural trends to generate the aesthetic of their times. Through careful observation, intensive research, experiments, and studies, documented in design journals and portfolios, designers should strive to create meaningful and personalised garments, cherished by customers for years.

Highly competitive fashion companies expect designers to constantly update their portfolios reflecting changes in society, technology and trends. The designer's portfolio is the ultimate expression of their identity, capturing a sensibility, style, target customer, market and price point. Nothing is more important for a fashion company than to have a successful match between the company's business focus and the creative identity of their designer. A designer's portfolio is what companies rely on to assess this match, and get a glimpse into their own future. From cover to cover, the fashion portfolio is the summary of designer's creative achievements and it is impossible to overstate its significance.

FASHION IN PERSPECTIVE

1900s
The Gibson Girl

The Exposition Universelle held in Paris at the dawn of the new millennium showcased the industrialisation of a modern age. Against the backdrop stood the Gibson Girl, in her delicate swirling white lace skirts designed by Charles Frederick Worth, the grandfather of haute couture. Echoing the curvaceous lines of the popular Art Nouveau style, the favoured silhouette was that of a 'mature woman,' with her mono-bosom and 's-curve' shape accentuating a heavily corseted waist. Her long, romantic bishop sleeves and the modest, high-necked gowns were topped with long strands of pearls and wide-brimmed hats with ostrich plumes.

1900s Styles: Tailor-made suits, tea gowns
Colours: White, cream, pastel pink, pale blue, mauve
Fabrics: Lace, crêpe de chine, chiffon, tulle
Designers: Charles Frederick Worth, Jacques Doucet, Callot Soeurs, Drecoll, Redfern, Madame Paquin
Fashion Influences: Princess Alexandra, The Gibson Girl, La Gazette du Bon Ton, Vogue, Harper's Bazaar
Artists: Giovanni Boldini, John Singer Sargent

A solid foundation in fashion history is immensely useful for many fashion designers when seeking inspiration, and an understanding of past styles allows young designers to communicate with other industry professionals. Learning the way that styles have changed throughout the past can improve one's ability to forecast future trends, and training the eye to notice historical trends in silhouettes, fabric, colour stories and design motifs, can improve the ability to transform these ideas into new designs.

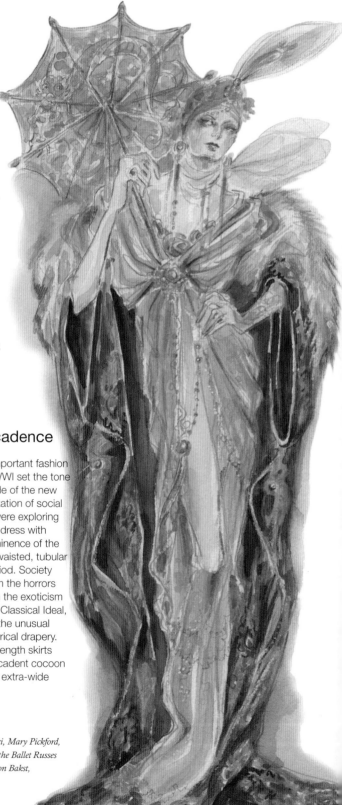

1910s
The Age of Decadence

Arguably the most important fashion influence in history, WWI set the tone for the second decade of the new century with the relaxation of social standards. Women were exploring a new-found ease of dress with the reduction in prominence of the corset and the high-waisted, tubular silhouettes of the period. Society found an escape from the horrors of daily wartime life in the exoticism of the Orient and the Classical Ideal, which showed up in the unusual textiles and asymmetrical drapery. The columnar, ankle length skirts were topped with decadent cocoon coats and turbans or extra-wide brimmed hats.

1910s Styles: The hobble skirt, Turkish pants, cocoon coats, turbans and fillets, parasols
Colours: Rich palette-reds, pinks, military greens
Fabrics: Hand painted, embellished silks, net, burn-out velvet
Designers: Paul Poiret, Lucile, Jean Lanvin, Mario Fortuny

Fashion Influences: Theda Bara, Pola Negri, Mary Pickford, Isadora Duncan, Mata Hari, Nijinsky and the Ballet Russes
Illustrators: Alastair, Aubrey Beardsley, Leon Bakst, Etienne Drian, Georges Lepape
Movies: Silent films like Cleopatra

1920s
The Flapper

With the post-war relaxation of social standards, new sporting activities and dances like the Tango and the Charleston had a profound affect on the modern 'jazz-age' generation. Women's suffrage was reflected in the most casual of dress seen in centuries. The ideal figure was 'the garçon', a youthful, energetic, boyish quality with skirts to the knees and bare arms. This new woman smoked cigarettes, bobbed her hair, and would never be seen in a corset. With the widespread use of the automobile came mobility and freedom, as well as time for recreational activities like tennis and golf.

1920s Styles: Robe de Style, Flapper dress, jersey separates, cardigan sweaters, tennis sweaters, cloche hat, gloves, silk stockings, long strands of pearls, costume jewellery, feather and fur boas, ankle-strap shoes; the bob and 'Eton' crop, rouged lips, pencilled eyebrows, the introduction of the zip
Colours: Sunset colours: sea green, dusty rose, slate blues and grays
Fabrics: Silk crêpe, silk georgette, beaded silks
Designers: Madeleine Vionnet, Coco Chanel, Hattie Carnegie, Sonia Delaunay, Jean Patou
Fashion Influences: Colleen Moore, Clara Bow, Claudette Colbert, Josephine Baker, Louise Brooks, Rudolph Valentino
Illustrators: Erté, J.C. Leyendecker
Fashion Photographers: George Hoyningen-Huene
Movies, Theatre and Books: Ziegfeld Follies, Charlie Chaplin, Aelita, the 'It Girl', Pandora's Box, The Great Gatsby

Fashion trends do not precisely follow the calendar, and many designers, celebrities, photographers and trends last far longer than one decade. The following is an attempt to identify the time period in which they were most influential, and help to organise major movements in social trends and the styles that followed them.

1930s
The Movie Star

Following the stock market crash of 1929, The Depression coloured the reality of fashion for many once-well-shod, but both the glamour of the Golden Age of Hollywood movies and the abstraction of surrealism were outlets for the nation. The boyish looks of the 1920s matured into a feminine silhouette, with a return to the natural waist, her curves emphasised by bias-cut dresses. This highly feminine decade featured flowers and ruffles, with demure Peter Pan collars and dropped hemlines. The width of her shoulders were dramatically emphasised by puffed or ruffled sleeves, giving a strong basis for the classical silhouettes.

1930s Styles: Bathing suits, bared-back evening gowns, envelope bags, fur capes and stoles, short, curly hair
Colours: Cream, peach, gold, champagne, chartreuse, shocking pink
Fabrics: Charmeuse, chiffon, nylon, floral prints, ruffles, bows, bias-cut drapery
Designers: Elsa Schiaparelli, Mainbocher, Madam Grés, Robert Piguet, Marcel Rochas, Elizabeth Hawes

Fashion Influences: Greta Garbo, Joan Crawford, Gloria Swanson, Marlene Dietrich, Ginger Rogers, Jean Harlow, Wallis Simpson, Anna May Wong
Illustrators: René Bouét-Williaumez
Fashion Photographers: Cecil Beaton, Horst P. Horst, Man Ray, Martin Muncasci, Edward Steichen, Erwin Blumenfeld
Movies: It Happened One Night, Gone with the Wind, The Women, Letty Lynton, Top Hat, She Done Him Wrong, Shanghai Express

1940s
Wartime

WWII put fashion in an unusually practical position, with women forced into factory work after the men had left for the front. Fabric rationing meant less fullness in the skirts and sleeves, and contributed to the slimmer, no-nonsense silhouettes and alternate materials like rayon. The 'make do and mend' campaign saw the recycling of garments and contrasting fabrics. With Paris occupied and London under siege, fashion saw a reliance on American designers and ready-to-wear for the first time. The feminine, romantic feeling of the 1930s sobered up to a mature, practical woman with her nipped-in waist, practical knee-length skirts, padded shoulders and long sleeves.

1950s
The New Look

The post-war return to domesticity saw a resurgence in high fashion, and the practical woman became a sophisticated lady in the 1950s. Her retreat to the home saw the return of the proper corseted waist, impractically full skirts, softly rounded shoulders and bracelet-length sleeves. A return to extravagant eveningwear and matched ensembles were a requirement for any well-dressed woman, but the Rockabilly and Beatniks also brought a youthful influence from the streets.

1950s Styles: Twinsets, pencil skirts, shirtwaist dress, cocktail dress, strapless ball gowns, 'the little black dress,' fur coats, stiletto heel, pearl necklaces, clutch purses, matching accessories, chignon hairstyles, gingham dresses, pedal pushers, Converse and Keds sneakers, preppy style

Colours: Jewel tones, neutrals
Fabrics: Wool tweed, cashmere, satin, taffeta, organza, nylon net, cotton piqué
Designers: Christian Dior, Cristobal Balenciaga, Pierre Balmain, Charles James, Norman Hartnell, Hardy Amies, Pauline Trigère, Hubert de Givenchy
Fashion Influences: Elizabeth Taylor, Audrey Hepburn, Grace Kelly, Marilyn Monroe, Sophia Loren, Gina Lollobrigida, Eva Peron, Evelyn Tripp
Illustrators: René Gruau, Coby Whitmore, Rene Bouché, Bernard Blossac
Photographers: Bill Brandt, Diane Arbus, William Klein, Cecil Beaton
Movies: Sabrina, Funny Face, The Seven Year Itch, Rebel Without a Cause, The Wild One, La Dolce Vita, Gentlemen Prefer Blondes, All About Eve, To Catch a Thief, Rear Window

1940s Styles: Practical workwear, austere tailored suits, wrap-around 'popover' dress, recycled knits
Utilitarian details: Patch pockets, epaulettes, larger buttons platform shoes, spectator shoes, fur stoles, shoulder-strap bags high-rolled hairstyles, snood hairnets, red lipstick, 'painted' stockings
Colours: Dark and dusty: utility blue, browns, grab green, beige
Fabrics: Wool, cotton, denim, rayon, seersucker, jersey, pinstripes, small scattered patterns
Designers: Norman Norell, Claire McCardell, Hattie Carnegie, Pierre Balmain, Edith Head, Adrian, Jacques Fath
Fashion Influences: Lauren Bacall, Lana Turner, Rita Hayworth, Kathryn Hepburn, Rosie the Riveter, Carmen Miranda
Illustrators: Eric, Alberto Vargas
Photographers: Louise Dahl-Wolfe, Lee Miller, Irving Penn
Movies: Gilda, Casablanca, It's a Wonderful Life, Rebecca

The rise of teenage culture and rock and roll during this decade had a lasting influence on fashion, as did the electronic age and the rise of suburban development, shopping malls, and the domestic use of washing machines.

1960s
The Mod

The woman who had been maturing over the last 30 years started over again in the 1960s, with a wide-eyed return to youthfulness and a naïve schoolgirl look colourfully influenced by Pop Art and Op Art. The look was unisex, with waistless sack dresses, short haircuts, and sleeveless tops. The mod styles of swinging London's Carnaby Street and King's Road reached the world along with The Beatles, The Who, The Rolling Stones, James Bond, and *The Avengers* in a 'British Invasion.' Hemlines shot up to the mini-skirt, showcasing colourful tights and go-go boots, and silver and metallic colours highlighted the inspiration of the Space Age. The free spirits of the decade saw the freedom of oral contraception and the Women's Lib movement, and politics met fashion in the Equal Rights Movement, at Woodstock and protests against the Vietnam War.

1960s Styles: Mini-skirts, shift dresses and jumpers, boxy coats, turtlenecks, bold top-stitching, oversized hardware, go-go boots, hipster style, 'bee-hive' and bouffant hair-dos, bob and wedge haircuts, cat-eyed eyeliner, pillbox hats, headbands

Colours and Prints: Mondrian-inspired colour blocks in primary colours, silver, white, Pucci prints

Fabrics: Futuristic: PVC, acrylic, polyester, crimplene, plastic discs, chainmail, clear plastic inserts.

Designers: André Courrèges, Paco Rabanne, Pierre Cardin, Mary Quant, Oleg Cassini, Ossie Clark, Rudi Gernreich, Guy Laroche, Bonnie Cashin, Emilio Pucci, Valentino

Fashion Influences: Twiggy, Jean Shrimpton, Edie Sedgwick, Peggy Moffitt, Penelope Tree, Catherine Deneuve, Brigitte Bardot, Jackie Kennedy

Illustrators: Andy Warhol, Bob Peak

Photographers: Richard Avedon, Norman Parkinson, David Bailey

Movies: Breakfast at Tiffany's, Belle de Jour, Barbarella, The Graduate, West Side Story

1970s
From Hippie to Disco

With the Vietnam War hovering overhead, the protesting, disco-generation embraced personal politics with free love and flower power. Multi-cultural influences were strong, with a dreamy nostalgia and interest in folkloric and vintage styles. The romantic, neo-Art-Nouveau chic of 'The Biba Look' was inexpensive and available to the masses via mail order. This accessible, handmade or ethnic natural look met the Studio 54 hip-hugger waists, flared pants, collared shirts and shirtwaist dresses of the Disco era.

1970s Styles: Trouser suits, ready-to-wear, t-shirts, maxi-dresses, A-line skirts, hotpants, bell bottoms, jumpsuits, craft revival, knitted hats and scarves, platform shoes, long, straight, centre-parted hair

Colours and Prints: Earthtones, Missoni patterns, floral prints

Fabrics: Polyester, lycra, brushed wool, corduroy, tweed, suede, oversized plaids

Designers: Yves Saint Laurent, Halston, Zandra Rhodes, Perry Ellis, Anne Klein, Diane von Furstenberg, Betsey Johnson, Kenzo

Fashion Influences: Farah Fawcett, Lauren Hutton, Angelica Houston, Olivia Newton-John, Angela Davis, Bianca Jagger, Jerry Hall, Patti Smith, ABBA, David Bowie, T. Rex

Illustrators: Kenneth Paul Block, Robert Melendez, Robert Passantino

Photographers: Guy Bourdin, Helmut Newton

Movies: Annie Hall, Love Story, Bonnie and Clyde, Taxi Driver, Saturday Night Fever, The Godfather

The liberated woman entering the workforce was casual and sporty, embracing trouser suits and ready-to-wear ensembles.

1980s
The Power Suit

The economic boom of the 80s saw the working girl in big hair, stilettos and power suits. Money, power and sex were buzzwords and the drive for success and social status was seen in the Yuppie phenomena. While the Cold War raged on, fashion also saw the influence of non-western designers with the 'Japanese Invasion.' Streetwear was influenced by boombox culture and the obsession with body image brought leotards and legwarmers to mainstream fashion. As a revolt against the flashy disco style and music, new trends emerged – the Punks, New Romantics, New Wave, Goths, and Heavy Metal styles paved the way for many subcultures.

1980s Styles: Mini-skirts, big frilly dresses, the designer bag, slouch socks, Ray-Ban sunglasses; bondage, slashing, safety pins, acid-wash jeans; leotards, leggings, loose shirts and sweaters, oversized jackets, sleeping-bag coats, shoulder pads, tracksuits, headbands, Reebok hype, strong makeup, oversized plastic jewellery, Swatch watches
Colours and Prints: Navy, black, purple, fuchsia and neon yellow, tie-dyes, splash paint prints
Fabrics: Spandex, lamé, seré, raw silk, woollen broadcloth, cotton terry, raw silk, bleached denim
Designers: Claude Montana, Thierry Mugler, Norma Kamali, Jean-Paul Gaultier, Vivianne Westwood, Versace, Azzedine Alaïa, Rei Kawakubo, Yohji Yamamoto, Issey Miyake, Comme de Garçons, Romeo Gigli, Sonia Rykiel

Fashion Influences: Madonna, Princess Diana, Grace Jones, Tina Turner, Cher, Ivana Trump, the 'Brat Pack', Michael Jackson, Brooke Shields
Illustrators: Antonio, Mats Gustafson, Zoltan, Tony Viramontes, Steven Stipelman, Stavrinos
Photographers: Nan Goldin, Bruce Weber, Herb Ritts, Patrick Demarchellier, Sarah Moon
Movies and TV: Flashdance, Desperately Seeking Susan, Working Girl, Dynasty, Dallas, Miami Vice, Blade Runner, Blue Velvet, Pretty in Pink, Scarface

1990s
Grunge and Glamour

The world exploded with the global connectivity brought by the Internet and the availability of cheap designer goods at factory outlets and discount stores. West Coast style dominated with the influence of surfers, skaters, and Grunge. Japan continued to be an influence, along with Utility Chic, Gypsy Style, Cyberpunk, Business Casual and American Sportswear. The subcultures that started in the 1980s blossomed as 'Style Tribes' in the 90s: Hip-hop, Rap, Ravers, Cyberpunks, Emo, Retro and 'Heroin chic.'

1990s Styles: The 'dressed down' look of baseball caps, cargo pants, plaid flannel shirts, long loose floral skirts, jeans, t-shirts, hoodies, oversized sweaters tied around the waist, Doc Martens, Victorian granny boots, platform shoes, tattoos, body piercings, the 'Rachel' hairdo, the Wonder Bra, yoga pants, athletic footwear such as Adidas, Nike, Fubu
Colours: Red, navy, mixed patterns, plaids and stripes, khaki and beige
Fabrics: Ink-jet printing, laser cutting, more sophisticated synthetic fabrics, distressed denim, cotton flannel, canvas, fleece, sandwashed silk
Designers: Marc Jacobs, Anna Sui, Sean John, Calvin Klein, Helmut Lang, Gucci, Tommy Hilfiger, Miuccia Prada, Martin Margiela, 'The Antwerp Six': Ann Demeulemeester, Walter Van Beirendonck, Dirk Van Saene, Dries Van Noten, Dirk Bikkembergs, Marina Yee

Fashion Influences: Courtney Love, Kurt Cobain, Cindy Crawford, Naomi Campbell, Christy Turlington, Linda Evangelista, Stephanie Seymour, Tyra Banks, Julia Roberts
Illustrators: Thierry Perez, Kareem Iliya, Ruben Toledo, Francois Berthoud, Joe Eula
Photographers: Mario Sorrenti, Juergen Teller, Corrine Day, David LaChapelle, Annie Leiboviz, Steven Meisel, Peter Lindbergh
Movies: Singles, Reality Bites, Pulp Fiction, Friends, My So-Called Life, Clueless, Interview with a Vampire,

2000s
Urban Minimalism

The 2000s were dominated by the fallout from 9/11 and the war in Iraq. Internationalism and global commerce influenced the look of the environmentally-conscious world traveller. The 'Style Tribes' of the 90s continued into 'Fusion Fashion,' incorporating new styles from Boho and Vintage looks, Harajuki and Lolita fashion, and the American Pioneer revival. This eclecticism mixed with a pragmatic style characterised by minimalism, understated beauty, androgyny, easy layers and practical fashion. Celebrities with their brands and pop-cultural influence dominated the fashion world, while high-end designers brought their vision and expertise to the mass commercial market.

2000s Styles: Low-rise skinny jeans, harem pants, distressed knits, crop-tops, Calvin Klein underwear, understated beauty and accessories
Colours: Subdued and neutral colours, shades of beige, gray and flesh tones
Fabrics: Organic fibres, nanotechnology and innovations in fabric treatments
Designers: Jil Sander, Céline, Stella McCartney, Francisco Costa, Michael Kors, Gucci, Miuccia Prada, Christian Louboutin, Nicolas Ghesquiére, Alexander McQueen

Fashion Influences: Kate Moss, Gisele Bündchen, Karolína Kurková, Doutzen Kroes, Agyness Deyn, Lily Donaldson, Tim Gunn, the Olsen Twins, Gwen Stefani
Illustrators: Jason Brooks, Sara Singh, David Downton, Tina Berning, Eduard Erlikh
Photographers: Nick Knight, Craig McDean, Mario Sorrenti, Patrick Demarchelier
Movies and TV: Zoolander, The Devil Wears Prada, Memento, Babel, Sex and the City
Reality television: American Idol, America's Next Top Model

2010s
Eclectic Chic

It may be challenging to identify the look of a decade when you're still in the middle of it, but so far, the fashion for the 2010s are eclectic and decadent, and showcase a personalised, individual style. The post-McQueen world of fashion is all about freakish, theatrical fantasy and storytelling, with an edgy, over-the-top take on historicism and tribalism. There is a dark, macabre sexuality to the diverse ornament of unique, mixed-matched styles. This time-travelling aesthetic likes to combine vintage and contemporary pieces, body art and the collaging of different markets, seasons and street styles.

2010s Styles: Leather jackets, tattoos and body art, layered belts and necklaces; mixing evening with activewear; corsets, bandages, lingerie worn on the outside
Colours and Prints: Black and dark metallics, neon and techno colours, tribal and neo-baroque prints
Fabrics: Textures and unravelling knits, mesh, net, tulle, neoprene, memory foam, gems, stones and oversized beads, long hair fur, leather and skins
Designers: Rick Owens, Gareth Pugh, Riccardo Tisci, Rad Hourani, Oliver Theyskens, Fendi, Alber Elbaz, Sophia Kokosalaki, Haider Ackermann, Balmain, Viktor & Rolf, Sandra Backlund, Rodarte
Fashion Influences: Kate Middleton, Lady Gaga, Daphne Guinness, Dita Von Teese, Bar Refaeli, Beyoncé, Victoria Beckham, Kim Kardashian
Illustrators: Daniel Egneus, Amelie Hegardt, Stina Perssons, Laura Laine, Cecilia Carlstedt, Petra Dufkova
Photographers: Steven Klein, G.L. Wood, Mikael Jansson, Mertalas, Paolo Roversi, Tim Walker
Movies and TV: Pan's Labyrinth, Game of Thrones, Hunger Games, The Twilight Saga, True Blood

Illustrations by
Anna Kiper

FORECASTING FASHION TRENDS

Fashion forecasting services predict future trends in colour, fabrics, silhouettes, accessories and cosmetics by analysing global cultural movements, changes in economy, technologies and consumer behaviour. Fashion companies use this vital information in order to stay on target with their design developments, and to ensure sales goals.

Fashion trend forecasting came into being early in the 1970s when European ready-to-wear eclipsed the traditional role that Paris haute couture had played for over a century. A handful of designers in the French fashion capital continued to issue formal dictates of silhouette, textiles and colour each season and the world blindly followed their lead. What had begun with Charles Frederick Worth in the 1860s, ended with the advent of Kenzo, Sonia Rykiel, Karl Lagerfeld and other young ready-to-wear designers who shook up the establishment with a variety of renegade fashion statements that suited young baby boomer consumers. Soon, more established designers, notably Yves Saint Laurent, followed suit. The American fashion industry took note and followed these new, more pop-culture-street-style sensitive designers who were tuned in to the younger generations.

Fashion has always been about change; about the eye becoming saturated with the current styles and becoming intrigued with a fresh look, a new silhouette, fresh fabrics and different colours. That traditional swing of the fashion pendulum sped up considerably during the 'Youthquake' of the 1960s and continued to gain more momentum throughout the 1970s. That is when the Fashion Trend Forecast came into being. Projecting what would be in fashion 18–24 months ahead became a vital consideration to manufacturers and retailers who had to produce and sell whatever was going to be desired by fashion-conscious consumers who became quick-change artists.

A handful of small consultancy-type companies popped up, first in London and Paris, and then in New York and Los Angeles. Those companies included Promostyl, IM International, Dominique Peclers, Trend Union and others. They were created to provide forecasts of incoming trends. Because there was a genuine need for inspired creative thinking in advance of the trends, these companies were instantly successful, working with many major manufacturers and retailers. Their forecasts became self-fulfilling prophecies because their projections were acted upon, and therefore 'came true.' The demand for quick turnover of creative ideas was intense. Diana Vreeland, legendary fashion editor of *Vogue* said that she gave her readers what they wanted before they knew what they wanted. That is exactly what the best fashion trend forecasters gave their clients.

Because of the long lead-time required by fashion designers, fabric mills and manufacturers, most fashion trend forecaster's prediction are projected 18 to 24 months ahead. Sometimes unforeseen world affairs can affect the consumer mindset so much that forecasts need to be recast and altered to fit new circumstances. For example, when the stock market crashed in 1987, suddenly the lavish fashions of hot designer Christian Lacroix, a widely copied creator, were no longer coveted. His career faltered and never regained its momentum. During the Gulf War of 1990–91, again circumstances affected consumer psyches and the optimistic colour palettes that had been projected to sell in the spring of 1991 were out of synch with serious times. No sooner had colourists adjusted to the new somber mood then the short-term military action was over and downbeat colours were wrong. Fashion trend forecasters cannot foresee some events that change the course of history and therefore the course of fashion.

David Wolfe, Creative Director, The Doneger Group

Images from trend forecast, d.cipher fm

From the start of forecasting in the early 1970s to the first decades of the 21st century, the fashion industry has undergone seismic changes. Economic fluctuations, technological breakthroughs, demographic shifts — all have had great impact. Whereas the trend forecasts used to be considered 'creative input and inspiration,' the successful ones have been retooled as 'business strategy aids,' providing sound commercial guidance for future planning. Trend forecasts are now based on carefully analysed performance data, with the Internet as the major source of information and observation. The most demanded talent in the forecasting sector today is the ability to meld business acumen and creativity in projecting the future of fashion trends.

Some forecasting companies report on more than just the latest colours and silhouettes, they go to the roots of trend development, analysing social and economic changes in society. These reports often give a fuller picture of consumer behaviour, referring to lifestyle, beauty, accessories, and preferences in interior and product design.

STREET TRENDS

Street fashion is an authentic way of dressing that emerged in the urban environment through youth subcultures. Urban culture is reminiscent of tribal customs where members show their affiliation with a particular group through body decoration and clothes. Most contemporary urban trends appear as a rebellion against establishment and current social and economic norms.

Each significant street trend is associated with a particular look, attitude, music and, most importantly, life philosophy. For example, Punk style is not only identified by ripped clothes, spike-encrusted leather, mohawks, body piercing and loud aggressive rock music, but also with nihilistic and anarchistic views. Another prominent example is the revolt against the rigid Japanese society of the previous generations, the Lolita, Decora and Anime styles, allowing youth to partake in escapism and fairytale illusions. The avoidance of the 'suit and tie' fate cultivates childlike behaviour that accepts the carrying of toys, pacifiers, extravagent layering, mismatched clothes in contrasting colours, and cartoon costumes.

Street trends evolve constantly, passing and reviving as cultural and sociopolitical influences emerge. The New Romantics of the early 1980s evolved into the Goth and Emo of later decades. The original hippies of the 60s transformed into the New Age Traveler trend of late 80s. Hip-hop started as the Rude Boy trend that epitomised early urban pop culture.

Popular Steet Trends of the Past Decades:
1940s Zootie and Zazou
1950s Biker, Hipster, Beatnik,
        Teddy Boy, Rockabilly
1960s Mod, Psychedelic, Hippie
1970s Disco Glam, Punk
1980s Goth, Raver, Hip-hop
1990s Grunge, Cyberpunk
2000s Emo, Lolita

Japanese Lolita

Rap Glamour

Spontaneously emerged street trends are a prominent source of inspiration for commercial fashion, anxious to turn an authentic movement into hype for the latest fashion.

Fututistic Emo

Street Punk

Eccentric Style

Street trends find influence in, and are influenced by, underground and emergent music genres. For example, Zooties found their voice in swing music and Hippies through folk ballads.

Urban Goth

Anime Style

Uptown Chic

Hip-hop

Hip-hop originally influenced young urban males who adopted oversize t-shirts, baggy jeans, baseball caps (worn backwards or sideways) and weighty trainers. As the music's popularity rippled out into mainstream pop culture, so too did the fashion.

The fashion industry is divided into 'markets,' each identified by the garment quality, look, price, customer and purpose.

HAUTE COUTURE: At the top end of the fashion market, these garments are one-of-a-kind pieces created from the finest materials, with exclusive workmanship, and are often designed for a specific customer and event. In French, 'couture' means 'dressmaking' and takes its roots from the fashion house of Charles Frederick Worth. These days couture designers belong to the Chamber Syndicate, which sets specific rules and guidelines for its members. Brands include: Dior, Valentino, Chanel, Balmain, Lanvin, Nina Ricci, Christian Lacroix and Yves Saint Laurent.

DESIGNER: This category includes high-end, ready-to-wear clothes produced by well-known designers using superior fabrics, trims and furnishings. The refined look, tailored fit and top-quality garments target the sophisticated and affluent customer. Brands include: Armani, Prada, Céline, Donna Karan, Ralph Lauren, Calvin Klein, Jil Sander and Michael Kors.

YOUNG DESIGNER: This niche of the market belongs to up-and-coming designers that are well represented in high-end department stores and speciality boutiques. Focusing on trendy looks and using cutting-edge, innovative materials and technologies these designers appeal to a younger, fashion-conscious customer with a disposable income. Brands include: Derek Lam, Rodarte, Peter Som, Rag & Bone, Christopher Kane and Phillip Lim.

UPPER BRIDGE: Competitively priced, this market is geared toward a broader audience, still with relatively high incomes, and functions as a bridge between the 'designer' and 'better' categories. This category is represented by secondary lines of designer collections and some better quality, well-known European and American brands. Brands include: Max Mara, Elie Tahari, Anne Klein, Ellen Tracy, DKNY, Marc by Marc Jacobs, BCBG and Theory.

BRIDGE TO BETTER: Markets representing private label companies and more moderately priced, popular brands targeting a wider range of customers, including young professionals. These clothes are sold mostly in large department stores like Macy's and Lord & Taylor, and free-standing boutiques. Brands include: Club Monaco, Banana Republic, Zara, J.Crew and Jones New York.

CONTEMPORARY: Fast-paced companies, offering modern, trendy fashion items to a younger, status-conscious customer. These popular brands are aiming for edgy and innovative designer looks at more affordable prices. Brands include: Guess?, Bebe, Diesel, Juicy Couture, DKNY Jeans, CK Jeans, Abercrombie & Fitch, Free People and Miss Sixty.

MODERATE: Somewhat fashion-forward, widely available commercial brands often including adaptations of higher-priced labels and selling affordable merchandise in volume. This category appeals to more price-conscious customers across several age categories and social/economic statuses. Brands include: Gap, Express, H&M, Hollister and New Look.

BUDGET: This low-end market is focused on mass-production at very affordable price points for a wide range of ages and demographics. While aiming for a trendy look, these brands commonly compromise on the garment's fit and quality. Brands include: Forever 21, Wet Seal, Old Navy, Target and Kohl's. As a recent trend, high-end designers have been collaborating with budget brands to bring high-concept ideas to the mass market, for example, Missoni for Target, Vera Wang for Kohl's, Viktor & Rolf for H&M.

CUSTOMER AND MARKETS

Donna Karen, Autumn / Winter, 2012 / 13

Brand: BCBG
Style: Suvi jacket, fitted, crew neck, asymmetrical front zipper
Colour: Black
Fabric content: 70% polyester, 25% rayon, 5% spandex geometric pattern sequins embroidery
Price: $498

Brand: BCBG
Style: Roxy mini skirt
Colour: Black
Fabric content: 100% lamb leather Quilted leather, jersey trims, metal front zippers
Price: $198

SHOPPING REPORT

In-store retail reports are one of the most effective research tools. Seeing merchandise from recent runway shows presents an overview of the current market trends and informs the researcher of finishing techniques, garment construction details, and modern colour and fabric stories. Retail research should be documented through detailed sketches, notes describing colour, embellishments, fabric quality and content, as well as references to brand name and the garment's price.

CATEGORIES

Fashion products are divided into sectors to facilitate manufacturing, marketing and sales. The main categories include Womenswear, Menswear and Childrenswear. However, each of these categories are subdivided into specialities allowing companies to focus design and production on a smaller segment of the industry. These categories include: Evening Wear and Special Occasion, Coats and Suits, Sportswear and Separates, Knitwear, Outerwear, Activewear and Swimwear, Lingerie and Sleepwear.

SEASONAL DELIVERIES

Most large brands follow a common fashion calendar with six seasonal deliveries: Transition/ Early Fall, Fall, Holiday, Resort/Early Spring, Spring and Summer. However, some high-end labels focus mainly on Fall and Spring due to more expensive productions. Stores transition from one delivery to another, often with overlapping deliveries on the floor, for a smoother evolement in colour and silhouettes.

CUSTOMER

For every fashion label, targeting a clearly defined customer is a key element for successful sales. Visual imagery and lifestyle descriptions will reinforce the collection's focus on a particular customer, market and price point. Today, consumers often have new perceptions of age and style, buying across markets in order to create a unique personal look and self-image.

Older customer profile:
Retired artist, eccentric,
stylish and fashionable
despite her age. Lives
in the artsy suburbs
of London. Obsessed
with chunky jewellery,
trendy leather and
denim looks.

THE FASHION MUSE

Often designers have a vision of a muse while creating their collections. Models, actresses, celebrities, and fashion icons usually become a prominent inspiration for many designers in their creative process. Every detail is an inspiration — attitude, way of dressing, accessories, and makeup — all are evoked in future designs and styling. Fascinated by personal style and beauty, designers associate their collections with their muse, an image of the ideal customer.

ascot

inside-out hunting jacket

long-tailed shirt

knitted cap

hunting jacket

fair isle vest

jodhpurs

Designs developed through styling of a vintage jacket

The Muse: Maggie Norris, designer, entrepreneur, eclectic, elegant New Yorker, equestrian, socialite, world traveller, collector of art and antiques, lover of classical music and film noir. Maggie Norris' signature pieces are seen on this page.

handcrafted Indian belts

For years the eccentric style of Isabella Blow and Daphne Guinness inspired McQueen's theatrical collections. At the same time, Madonna as a sex symbol of the Grunge era, brought to life Jean Paul Gaultier's explicit inside-out lingerie collection, and the plain, girl-next-door look of Kate Moss influenced Calvin Klein's simplistic bare minimal look of the 90s.

pinstriped shirt

Capsule collection inspired by Maggie Norris' personal style.

By creating a narrative around the muse, designers stay focused on a specific lifestyle and personality that they refer to when selecting fabrics, colours and prints. The final collection should portray the general essence of the muse, becoming the designer's interpretation of the subject.

Popular Fashion Muses:
Jacqueline Kennedy
Princess Diana
Marlene Dietrich
Marilyn Monroe
Audrey Hepburn
Catherine Deneuve
Dita Von Teese
Daphne Guinness
Tilda Swinton

ANNA KIPER

When creating a concept for a collection, a designer seeks inspiration from many avenues. Personal aesthetic and style is shaped by various cultural encounters and world exploration.

Story boards

During the time of Napoleon, fashion was intricate and romantic for both men and women. Bonaparte's military attire was influential for fashion and the decorative arts. In the Napoleon collection, handcrafted, cut-away satin jackets and double-breasted velvet coats embellished with antiqued gold and silver were combined with Edwardian-era bespoke shirts and beaded cummerbunds to create a 'dandy' attitude.

In an attempt to create refined and unique pieces designers should never limit themselves to search engines while researching, but rather reference timeless art and history, and explore the treasures in antique and vintage shops. Creative influences range from nature to cultural sources — art, cinema, and literature spanning various eras. Referencing influential history such as iconic styles and significant figures from the past is invaluable. Once a designer's thoughts and research are fully compiled and documented in an inspiration journal, choices can be narrowed down and mood boards can be created.

Presentation created with vintage props

Hats by Albertus Swanepoel

In mood boards, designers aim to portray the elements of the collection: colours, textures, shapes, style lines and fabric swatches. After an idea is composed, sketches are created to show possible options and the collection begins to take on its own form.

At the turn-of-the-century, the Orient Express evoked an attitude of luxury and style with a flavour of a traditional Chinese watercolours and calligraphy.

Collections by Maggie Norris Couture.

Silk paintings, embroideries and illustrations by Anna Kiper

Lavish embroideries and hand-painted fabrics were influenced by journeys to the East passionately described in Shanghai Express with Anna May Wong in 1932.

23

DESIGN

A designer should have a unique voice; be original; see beyond the obvious; explore endlessly; follow intuition; communicate a big vision; and ultimately find a balance between creativity, dreams, fantasy and the realities of the commercial and utilitarian world.

CREATIVE PROCESS AND DESIGN TOOLS

Inspiration: The source of inspiration can come from various forms of art: music, film or architecture. It often comes from memories, feelings, emotions and associations. Design can also be influenced by familiar surroundings, ordinary objects, casual daily-life moments and observations.

Research: Detailed research should be conducted by carefully studying all aspects of the chosen inspiration. Sketches, snapshots, articles and notes should be placed in a journal as part of the preliminary design process.

Design: A crucial step in the design process is translating the inspiration into an actual design story, complete with colour, fabric and silhouette development. Finding the right words and associations in order to establish the connection between the chosen mood and the tangible elements of the collection (i.e. trims and garment details) are critical. Writing a brief description to verbalise the inspiration, helps turn abstract ideas into concrete designs.

This collection was developed using the following steps:

Step 1: Old brick buildings and deteriorated sidewalks of London are selected as the source of inspiration.

Step 2: Photographs of cracked concrete and brick are collaged and painted over, becoming an abstract work of art and a base for colour and textile development.

Step 3: Colours and textures of yarns for the hand woven tapestry are extracted from the rendered collages.

Step 4: Final silhouettes are composed through collage, using the tapestry photocopies, and emulating the deconstructed feeling of the initial inspiration.

1

2

ZEYING MARIA WANG

The design process for this woven tapestry collection is influenced by photographs and drawing studies of old London buildings and construction sites. Transparent photographs are superimposed on top of opaque images in order to create intersecting lines and planar shapes.

4

3

DESIGN JOURNAL

The design journal is a powerful, creative tool where artists can express their unique vision through visual collages, sketches and notes. A journal should capture a spectrum of thoughts, associations, memories and emotions, as well as become an archive of inspirational visuals. The professional journal should serve as a creative diary of daily research, reflecting the various steps of the design process.

This journal was created from an old book of novels with yellowing pages and fading text. Prior to collaging images, pages were soaked in water, air-dried and coffee stained to look thoroughly aged. Water soluble pens, nail polish and cotton balls were used to illustrate figures.

Bleeding stains and spills, stencilled lettering, and wrinkled pages with distressed edges taped with coloured vinyl lend a intense, rustic feel to the journal. Collaged yarns, layers of clear acetate and sprinkled shards of coloured plastic give dimension and an eclectic feel to the art work.

SCARLET HYE RIM JANG

The 'blue sea' was the inspiration for these pages. The scenes of the deep, wild sea were painted and collaged from memory. Draping studies and soft, open-weave swatches emulate the waves and evoke a sense of drama and the infinite.

Fabric swatches look as though they have been washed out by the sea and lend a serene, frayed quality.

OLGA BELY

Fabric collage
SCARLET JANG

CREATIVE THUMBNAILS

Designers communicate their ideas through draping, textile samples, collages, sketches and notes. Modern design sketches, commonly called thumbnails or croquis, are often a combination of all of these things. As an essential part of the creative process, thumbnails are usually placed in a design journal and strongly reflect the designer's aesthetic, intended customer, mood and narrative of the collection. While exploring design possibilities and style variations, thumbnails become a visual line-up of preliminary ideas, allowing designers to test garment silhouettes, proportions and details in a 2D format. Often quick, and partially developed, thumbnails are key for a cohesive collection of final looks with a nice flow in fabric, colour and style.

Collage, ink and bleach

OU MA

Thumbnails are small, simplified design sketches with a uniquely developed look, which becomes the prelude to the final presentation. Besides pencil and colour rendering, other popular techniques are used for thumbnail development, including fabric and paper collages; draping and 3D textile photomontages, as well as digital image manipulations.

Digitally-enhanced hand drawings

ZEYING MARIA WANG

3D paper collage

FEITONG LU

ANTHONY ARGENTINA

Watercolour and photomontaged draping studies

2D AND 3D THUMBNAILS

Some designers communicate their ideas through specific design sketches, thumbnails or croquis. Traditional design journals with detailed thumbnails, fabric swatches and preliminary drawing studies of garment details and functions are still very common in the fashion industry.

Journal pages include inspirational images, colour story, trims, suggestions for beauty and accessories. This design approach is mainly implemented through 2D drawings and flat sketch studies.

A series of design sketches based on the idea of mental anxiety and a need for over-protection. Grey, beige and nude act as camouflage in a modern city; our own skin blends with concrete, cement and aluminum. Padded, quilted and puffy fabrics serve as protection for hiding the body.

DIANA CHENG

Bubble wrap Jackets

Grommit

layered hood

Neck and head Protection

harness

Light weight waterproof

down filling

Exposed zipper

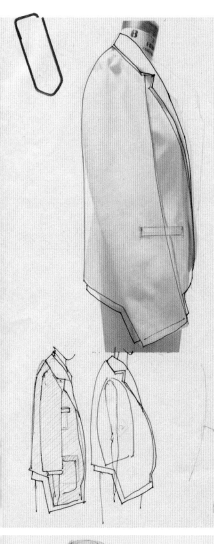

The 3D-design approach represents creative developments generated through draping and fabric manipulation, as well as deconstruction and reconstruction of existing garments, in order to illustrate a specific design idea.

The 3D-design process is more popular among designers with innovative, avant-garde ideas, as well as those who prefer to view their creative development in 360 degrees. Various snapshots of this creative process serve as an alternative thumbnails.

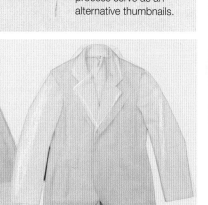

Fine artist Andrea Lopez Garcia's drawings were the inspiration for this design development, representing lines and shapes that define the core of an object. Based on the idea of transforming an artistic process into sartorial form, this design process involves a series of stylistic experiments to find correlations among different tailoring techniques. Numerous jackets were deconstructed and multiple lines were overlaid via digitised images to find stylistic correlations.

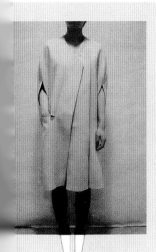 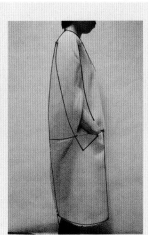 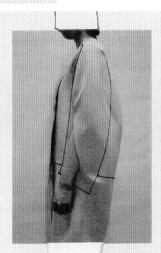 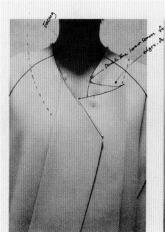 

JUN JUYEON HONG

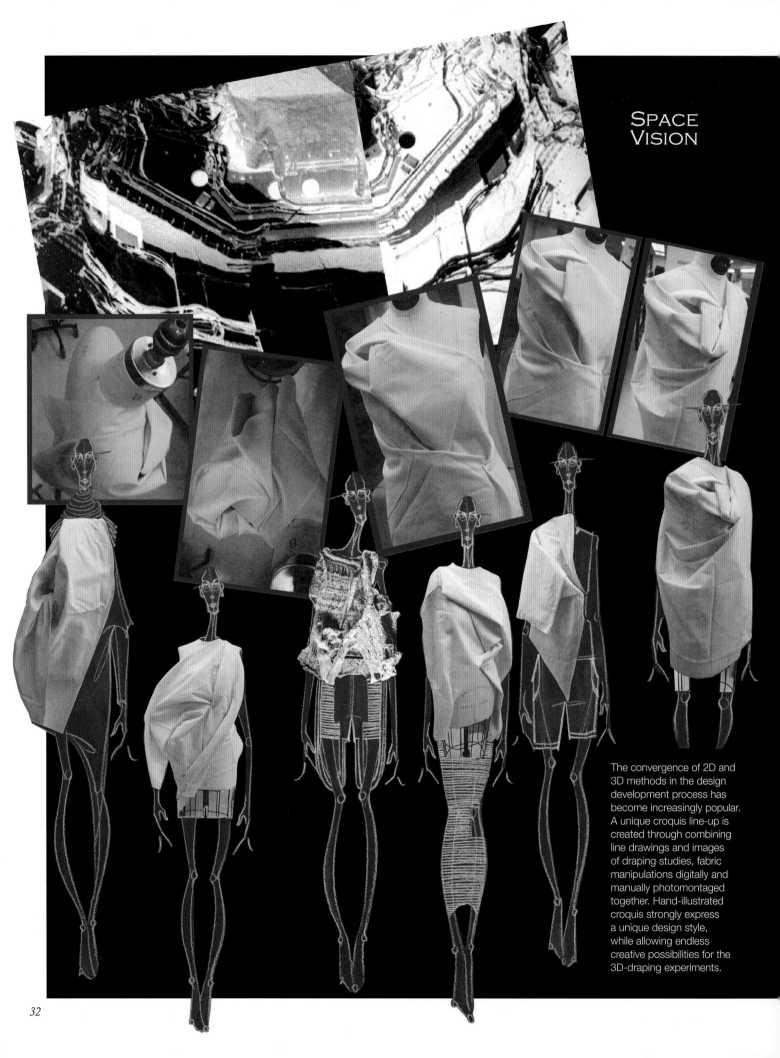

SPACE VISION

The convergence of 2D and 3D methods in the design development process has become increasingly popular. A unique croquis line-up is created through combining line drawings and images of draping studies, fabric manipulations digitally and manually photomontaged together. Hand-illustrated croquis strongly express a unique design style, while allowing endless creative possibilities for the 3D-draping experiments.

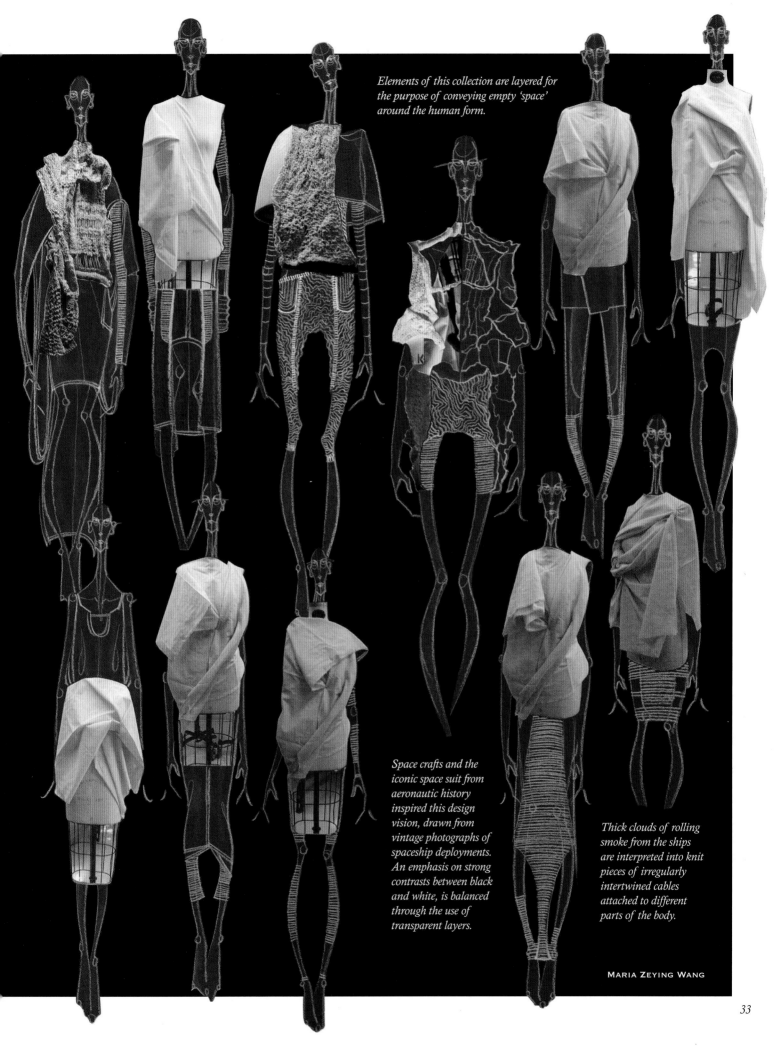

Elements of this collection are layered for the purpose of conveying empty 'space' around the human form.

Space crafts and the iconic space suit from aeronautic history inspired this design vision, drawn from vintage photographs of spaceship deployments. An emphasis on strong contrasts between black and white, is balanced through the use of transparent layers.

Thick clouds of rolling smoke from the ships are interpreted into knit pieces of irregularly intertwined cables attached to different parts of the body.

MARIA ZEYING WANG

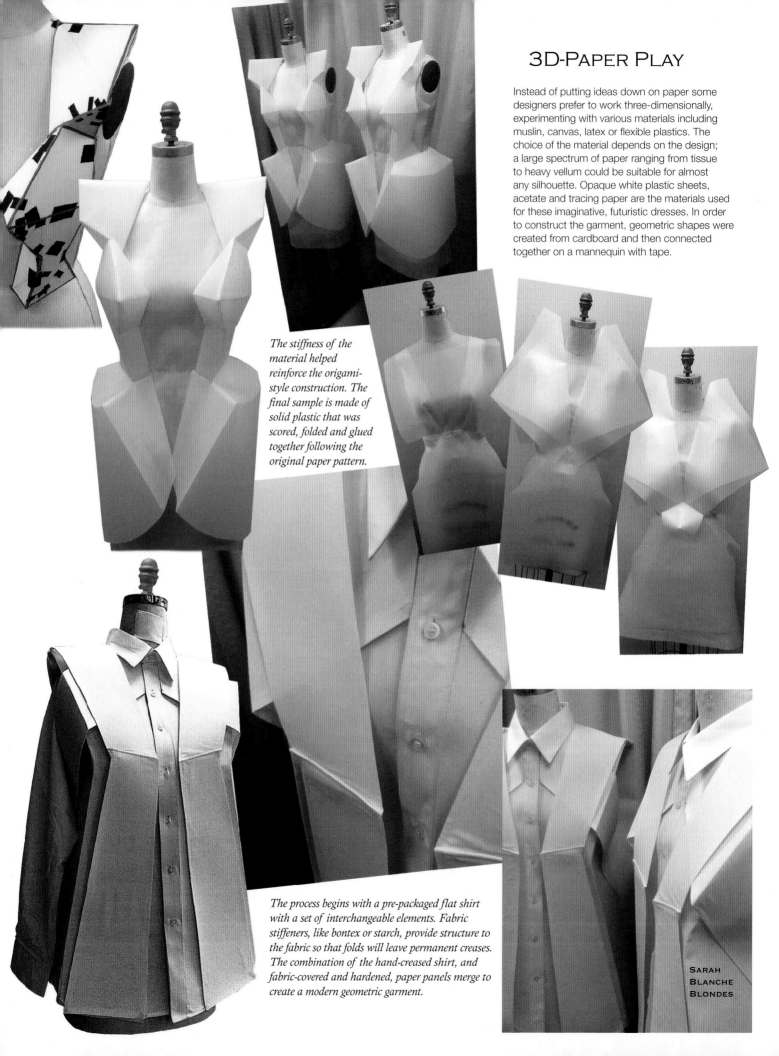

3D-PAPER PLAY

Instead of putting ideas down on paper some designers prefer to work three-dimensionally, experimenting with various materials including muslin, canvas, latex or flexible plastics. The choice of the material depends on the design; a large spectrum of paper ranging from tissue to heavy vellum could be suitable for almost any silhouette. Opaque white plastic sheets, acetate and tracing paper are the materials used for these imaginative, futuristic dresses. In order to construct the garment, geometric shapes were created from cardboard and then connected together on a mannequin with tape.

The stiffness of the material helped reinforce the origami-style construction. The final sample is made of solid plastic that was scored, folded and glued together following the original paper pattern.

The process begins with a pre-packaged flat shirt with a set of interchangeable elements. Fabric stiffeners, like bontex or starch, provide structure to the fabric so that folds will leave permanent creases. The combination of the hand-creased shirt, and fabric-covered and hardened, paper panels merge to create a modern geometric garment.

SARAH
BLANCHE
BLONDES

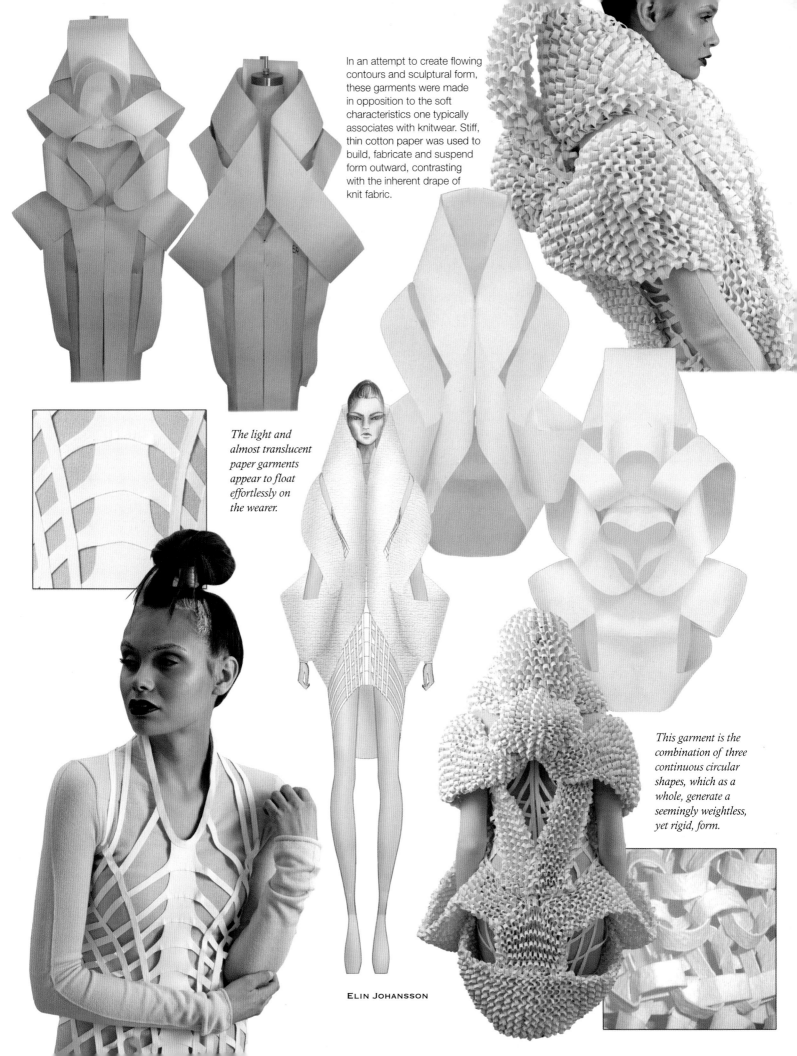

In an attempt to create flowing contours and sculptural form, these garments were made in opposition to the soft characteristics one typically associates with knitwear. Stiff, thin cotton paper was used to build, fabricate and suspend form outward, contrasting with the inherent drape of knit fabric.

The light and almost translucent paper garments appear to float effortlessly on the wearer.

This garment is the combination of three continuous circular shapes, which as a whole, generate a seemingly weightless, yet rigid, form.

ELIN JOHANSSON

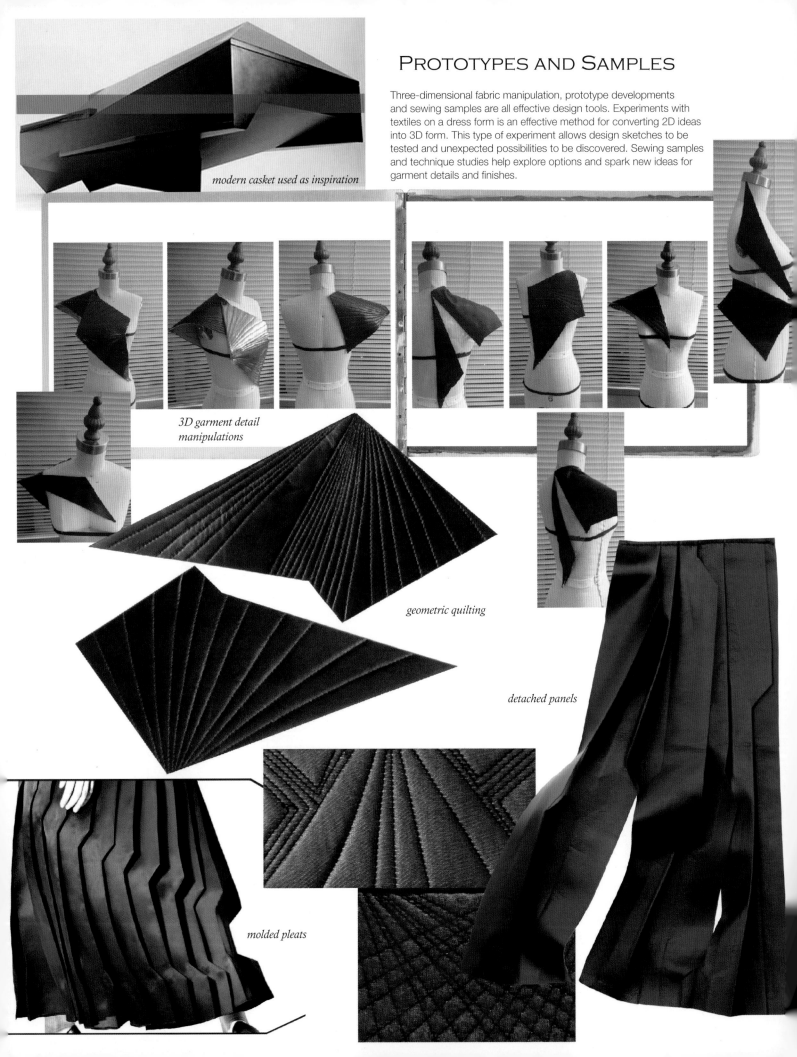

PROTOTYPES AND SAMPLES

Three-dimensional fabric manipulation, prototype developments and sewing samples are all effective design tools. Experiments with textiles on a dress form is an effective method for converting 2D ideas into 3D form. This type of experiment allows design sketches to be tested and unexpected possibilities to be discovered. Sewing samples and technique studies help explore options and spark new ideas for garment details and finishes.

modern casket used as inspiration

3D garment detail manipulations

geometric quilting

detached panels

molded pleats

The literal manipulation of the inspiration image resulted in the innovative pleats developed through paper pattern.

Inspired by the loss of a loved one, this collection symbolises the idea of letting go, moving forward in both life and design. The reinvention of traditional sewing techniques resulted in adapting the details from the pleated and quilted interior of the casket. Laser cutting added an additional dimension to the pleats while creating dimension, body and depth. Silhouette evolution resulted from drapings and manipulations on a dress form, engendering ideas for various design details.

irregular pleats

juxtapositioned pleats

box pleats with decorative stitching

JOSEPH SINGH

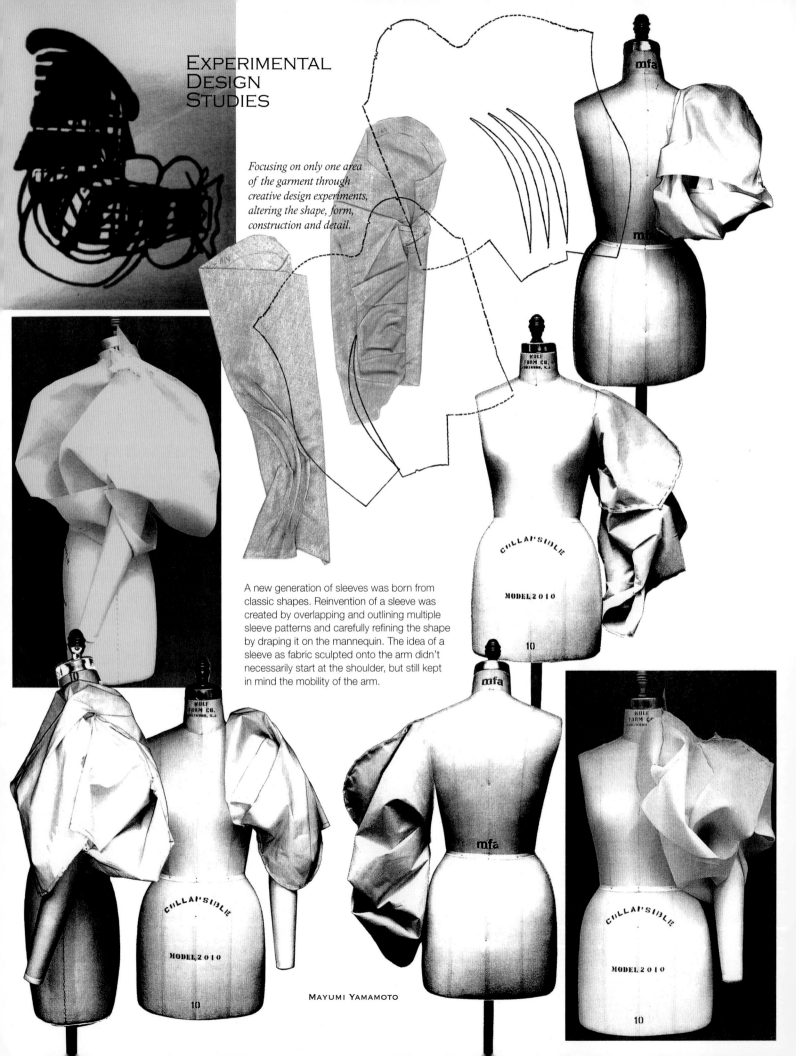

EXPERIMENTAL DESIGN STUDIES

Focusing on only one area of the garment through creative design experiments, altering the shape, form, construction and detail.

A new generation of sleeves was born from classic shapes. Reinvention of a sleeve was created by overlapping and outlining multiple sleeve patterns and carefully refining the shape by draping it on the mannequin. The idea of a sleeve as fabric sculpted onto the arm didn't necessarily start at the shoulder, but still kept in mind the mobility of the arm.

MAYUMI YAMAMOTO

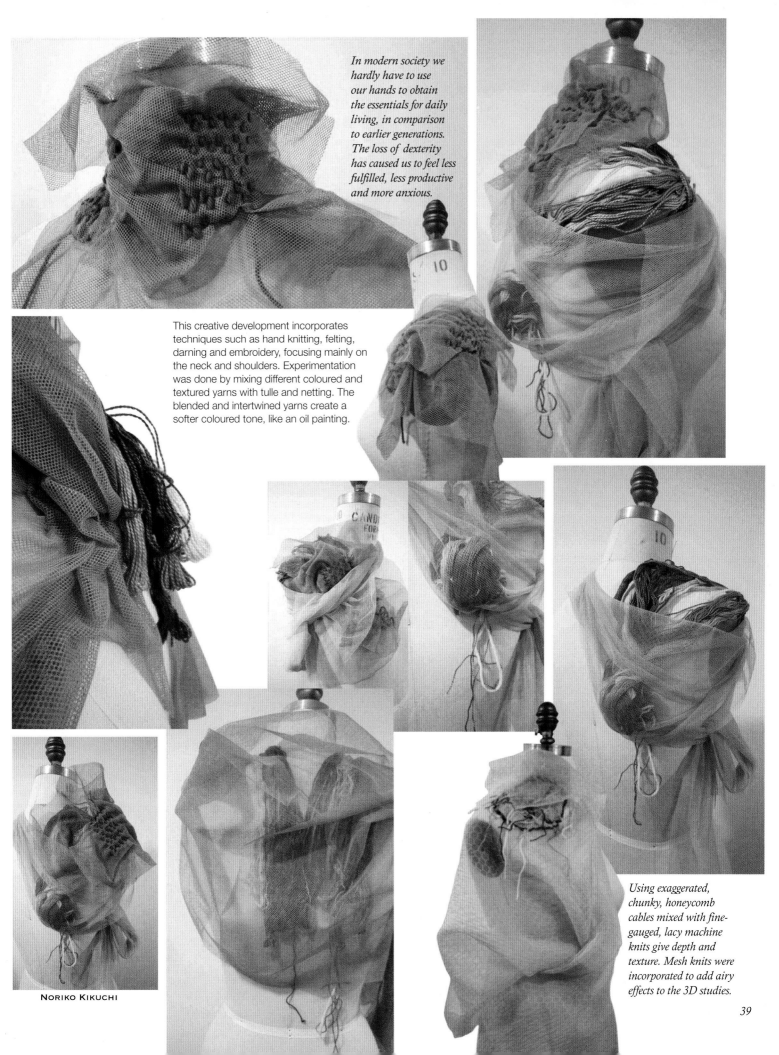

In modern society we hardly have to use our hands to obtain the essentials for daily living, in comparison to earlier generations. The loss of dexterity has caused us to feel less fulfilled, less productive and more anxious.

This creative development incorporates techniques such as hand knitting, felting, darning and embroidery, focusing mainly on the neck and shoulders. Experimentation was done by mixing different coloured and textured yarns with tulle and netting. The blended and intertwined yarns create a softer coloured tone, like an oil painting.

Using exaggerated, chunky, honeycomb cables mixed with fine-gauged, lacy machine knits give depth and texture. Mesh knits were incorporated to add airy effects to the 3D studies.

NORIKO KIKUCHI

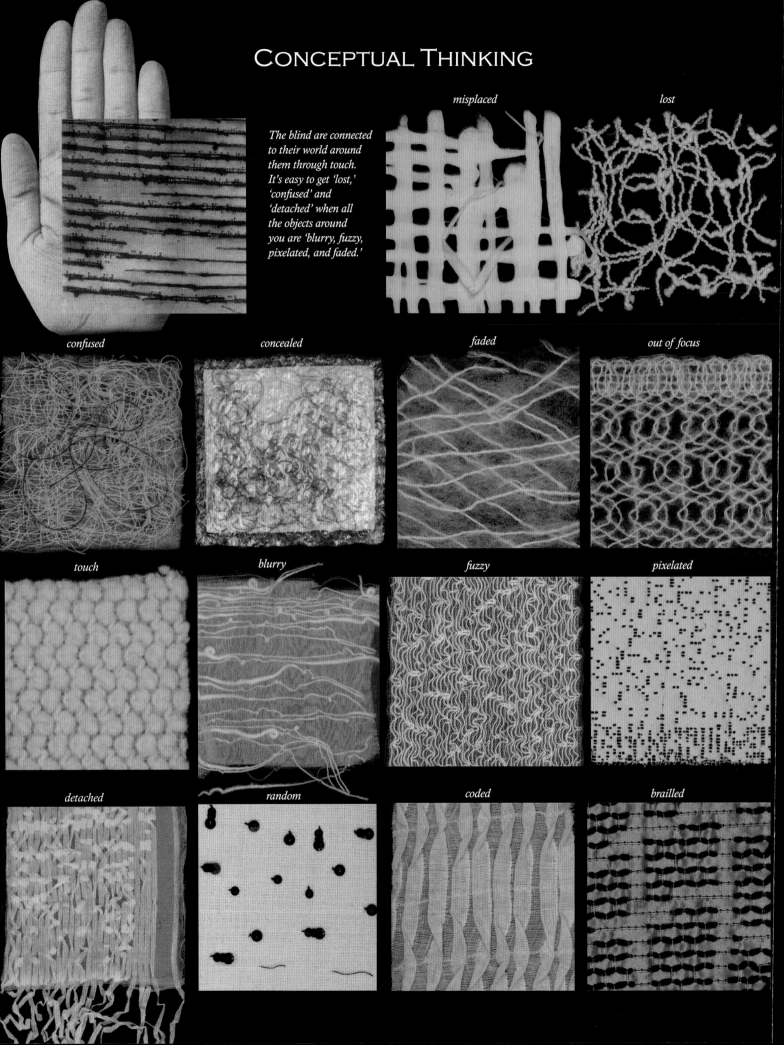

CONCEPTUAL THINKING

The blind are connected to their world around them through touch. It's easy to get 'lost,' 'confused' and 'detached' when all the objects around you are 'blurry, fuzzy, pixelated, and faded.'

misplaced

lost

confused

concealed

faded

out of focus

touch

blurry

fuzzy

pixelated

detached

random

coded

brailled

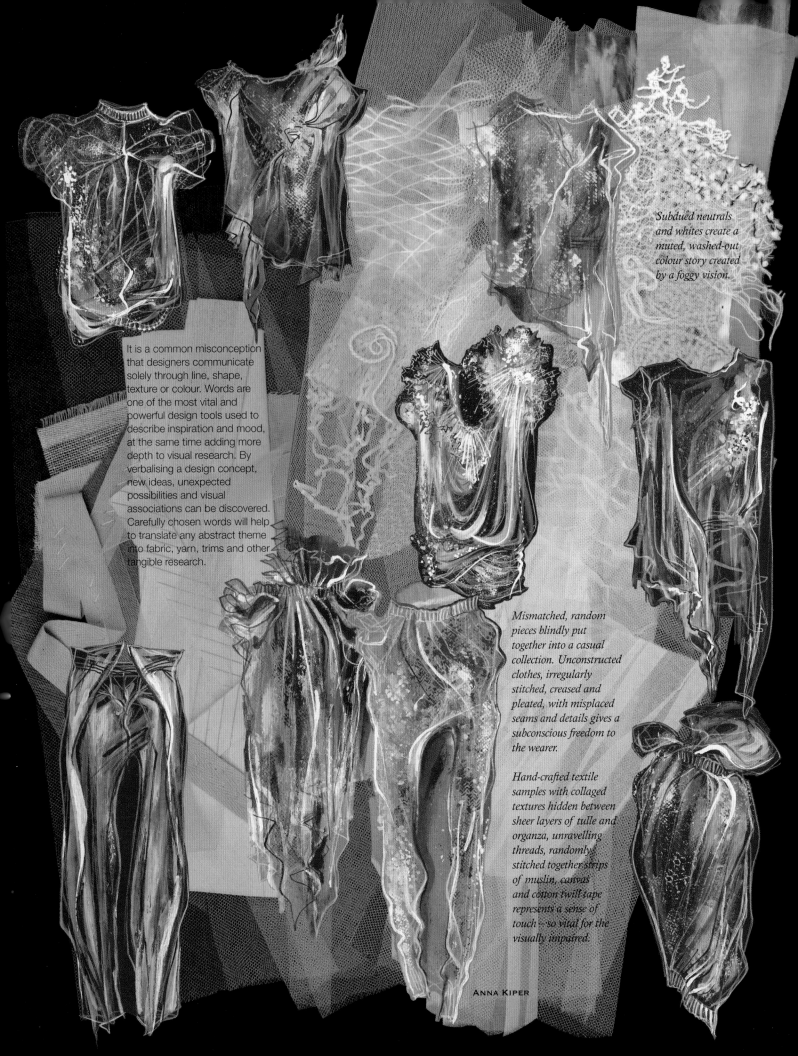

Subdued neutrals and whites create a muted, washed-out colour story created by a foggy vision.

It is a common misconception that designers communicate solely through line, shape, texture or colour. Words are one of the most vital and powerful design tools used to describe inspiration and mood, at the same time adding more depth to visual research. By verbalising a design concept, new ideas, unexpected possibilities and visual associations can be discovered. Carefully chosen words will help to translate any abstract theme into fabric, yarn, trims and other tangible research.

Mismatched, random pieces blindly put together into a casual collection. Unconstructed clothes, irregularly stitched, creased and pleated, with misplaced seams and details gives a subconscious freedom to the wearer.

Hand-crafted textile samples with collaged textures hidden between sheer layers of tulle and organza, unravelling threads, randomly stitched together strips of muslin, canvas and cotton twill tape represents a sense of touch – so vital for the visually impaired.

ANNA KIPER

WORDS AND DESIGN

A designer's research can follow many different avenues and be extensive as well as varied. In the end, however, research should focus on a single idea or perhaps a single image or word.

Original photo taken in the park

My secret door

Cutouts from original image layered into a pattern

The inspiration for the 'Secret Door' collection came from a photo of leaves with an opening beyond, which sparked the designer's imagination into envisioning a passageway into another world.

Original image transformed into a negative

hidden

Laser-cut fabrics imitating the contours of the leaves

layers

Words are used to describe the images; images are created to illustrate the words.

Transformed

ELSA ELLIES

The original photograph is a stolen moment, observed and captured as the light glimmered through the leaves. The graphic outline was amplified with the contrasting sizes of foreground leaves to background. The image is translated into abstraction through negative exposure, stencils, cutouts and juxtapositions. This process then transfers the photograph into textiles.

Some designers go beyond the idea of simply listing related words; they actually capture the mood of their collection in a beautifully composed paragraph.

An original poem serves as the storyline and inspiration for this collection, helping to create a surreal and magical mood.

camouflaged

dark

Tranquil

exposed

The secret door
My secret passage
Where I hear nothing
My escape

My secret passage
Dark secrets
My dark secrets
My secret door

TEXTILES AND MOOD

Screen printing on canvas, laser-cut leather and felt, stitchery and fabric collage techniques were used to express the mysterious mood of the collection.

laser-cut leather

digitally printed

cut felt

screen printed

deconstructed knit

stitchery

heat transferred

My secret passage
Dark secrets
My dark secrets
My secret door

From the orginal photograph featured on the previous page, the 'canopy of leaves' imagery has reached the final design phase.

ELSA ELLIES

EE

Escapism is a desire for solitude where barriers are broken down, we are naked and vulnerable, and simply exposing our true selves. This collection gravitates towards lighter weight, loosely woven wool, cashmere and organza to create a sense of vulnerability. The shapes of leaves were laser cut from leather, based on a black and white photo of a canopy of leafs. When the leaf samples are layered they resemble a passageway to a place where one can simply be free.

STORY AND PROCESS

The design process often resembles a vibrant and captivating story. The concept emerges, as the narrative unravels and evolves, through creative design developments using textile manipulations, drapings, sketches and notes.

Deep exploration of a subject also involves expanding on a story through brainstorming and mind maps. Mind maps express thinking patterns and ideas through free associations and organically linked words that are relevant to the design inspiration.

The 'Untouchable' knitwear concept collection comes from a private personal experience, an unexpected accident that interrupted normal life. Photographs of open wounds started the design process and are threaded throughout the collection. The wounds are represented in several forms such as burned edges, unravelled knit swatches and bleached sketches. Literally, they are broken and unfinished textile samples and design details, yet they represent the breakdown of both internal and external health.

As physical pain grows and invades other parts of the body, as shown in various versions of jacquard and intarsia patterns, it reaches mental and emotional chaos in an understated and indefinable way.

OU MA

Sketching techniques and media are mixed in an elegant manner in order to interpret the depth of spiritual pain. In the final stage of the collection, the designs imply that by loosening up the mind and forgetting the pain, healing can become possible from deep within.

Strong visual and emotional impact was created by magical design images and photography by Sarah Moon, deconstructed with bleach and turned edges.

By breaking down the long and unstable healing process into several stages, this knitwear-concept design collection deeply explores the status of mental disturbance and the infinite progression of emotional recovery. While physical pain has an end point, emotional trauma expands without boundaries and has no definite conclusion.

OU MA

CONCEPTUALISING COLOUR

Colour can be conceptualised
as part of the design process
and an entire philosophy can be
extracted from a single colour.
It can be an emotional foundation
for a collection, and other concepts
can emerge from the colour, such
as limitless space, eternity
and emptiness.

WHITE

White symbolises the
concept of 'emptiness,'
and the absence of
colour and yet it contains
the whole spectrum of
shades within.

*Creative studies using semi-transparent, fine-knitted textiles
express the complexity of white. A needle-punching technique
was used to fuse several fabrics together, as well as to connect
knits with woven mesh fabrics.*

NORIKO KIKUCHI

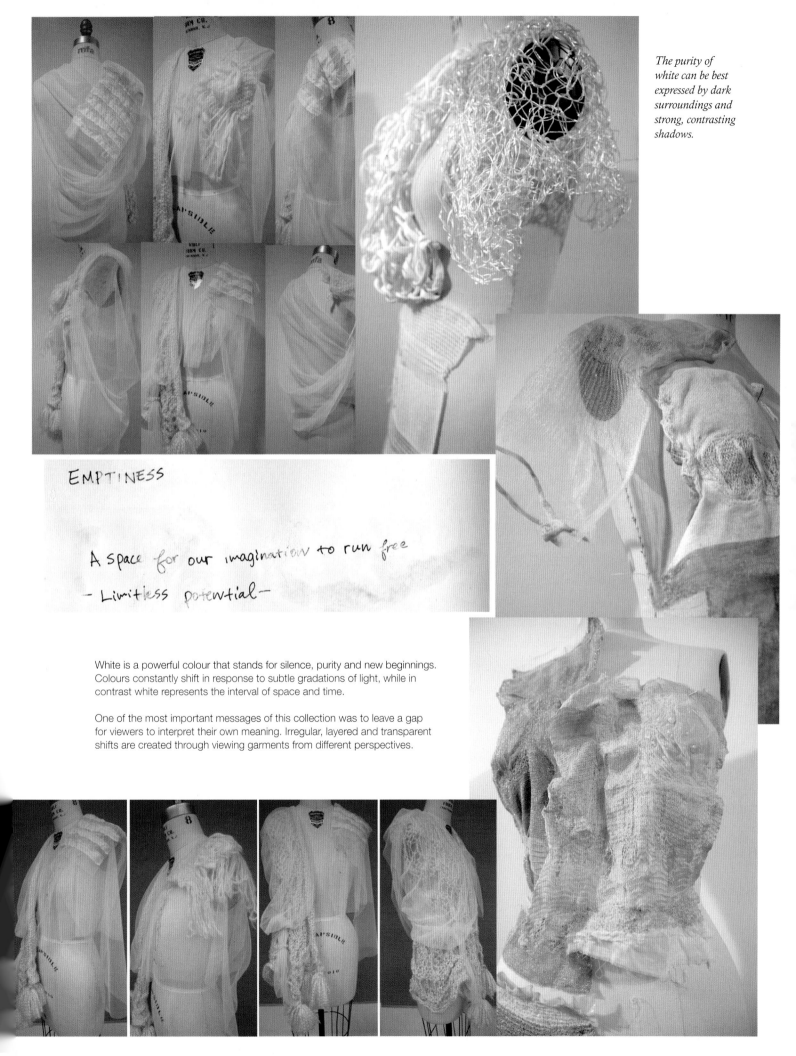

The purity of white can be best expressed by dark surroundings and strong, contrasting shadows.

EMPTINESS

A space for our imagination to run free
– Limitless potential –

White is a powerful colour that stands for silence, purity and new beginnings. Colours constantly shift in response to subtle gradations of light, while in contrast white represents the interval of space and time.

One of the most important messages of this collection was to leave a gap for viewers to interpret their own meaning. Irregular, layered and transparent shifts are created through viewing garments from different perspectives.

FORM AND PERSPECTIVE

Fashion is a combination of science and art. Design studies are a form of experimentation that may not lead to wearable garments but are still important for moving the design forward.

Williamsburg Bridge (left)

Queensborough Bridge (below)

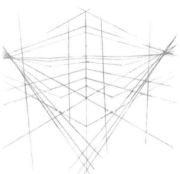

Inspiration for this abstract design development was derived from the invention and use of perspective in architecture and bridge construction. Indepth research of New York City's skyline, bridges, buildings and streets was an attempt to transform architectural qualities into 3D sartorial forms. Shapes and lines were created by using paper origami, and mapping them on to body forms. Thread lines were superimposed in various directions on muslin bodices, imitating random patterns created by bridge straps. Research and design processes do not necessarily lead to a finished collection, but can often remain as a sophisticated concept.

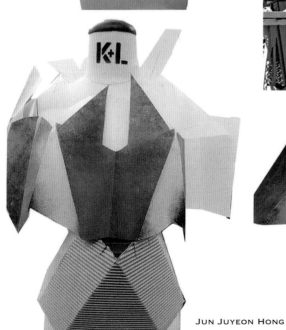

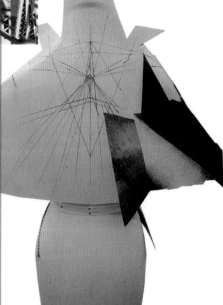

JUN JUYEON HONG

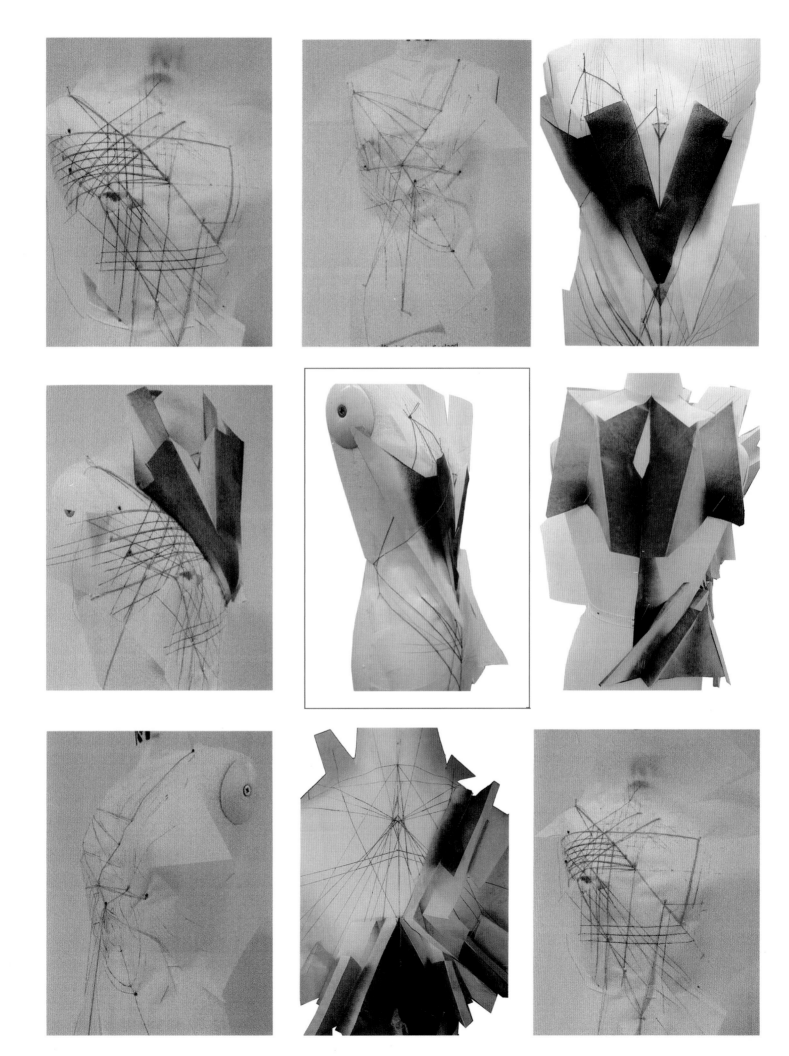

DESIGN APPROACHES

Some designers can be categorised into distinct groups, each one expressing a significant signature style. With time, designers grow creatively and evolve in their vision, and at various stages of their career they can be associated with different design approaches.

The Sculptors

Drawing their inspiration from modern architecture, geometrical sculptures, shapes and forms of the human body and anatomical lines, sculptors design in a 3D manner. They build structures out of fabric, focusing on negative and positive spaces created by cutouts and fabric blocking. Sculptors select fabrics for their ability to build and maintain shapes, often created through complex construction such as seaming, darting, inserts and undercuts. Sculptors often work without preliminary design sketches, forming ideas through spontaneous draping and instantaneous fabric manipulations. In some instances these designers drape the fabric directly, skipping the preliminary muslin or paper pattern stages, allowing the fabric to speak for itself.

Calvin Klein / Francisco Costa	Gianfranco Ferré
Geoffrey Beene	Balenciaga
Isabel Toledo	Ralph Rucci
Azzedine Alaïa	Narciso Rodriguez

Sculpted wool dress by Calvin Klein, Spring / Summer 2009

The Sensualists

The sensualists' creativity is mainly sparked by the arts, historical references, fantasy, dreams and illusions, and often is driven by feelings and intuition. Their instinctual and emotional approach allows them to trust their visions. A sensualist's collection often encompasses layers and layers of abstract information that ultimately materialises into tangible garments. They embrace opulent fabrics rich in colour and texture, and rely on embellishments, trims, and accessories to create styles. Sensualists select specific silhouettes and design details in order to set a particular mood creating theatrical drama and romance. Beading, embroidery, lace, brocades and iridescent fabrics help further emphasise the effects.

Alexander McQueen	Oscar de la Renta
Christian Lacroix	Caroline Hererra
Valentino	John Galliano

Historically-inspired velvet jacket by Alexander McQueen, Autumn / Winter 2008 / 09

The Rebels

The rebels are the barometers of society, constantly pushing boundaries and changing preconceptions. These designers push limitations and still find a balance between conformity and eccentricity, and move fashion forward by questioning traditional thinking and reacting to societal issues. Designing with the sixth sense and intuition, with the ability to see beyond the obvious, rebels challenge their audience by using unconventional, eccentric elements in their garments. Beauty and sensuality are subjective or even irrelevant for the rebels. They use clothes as a means for expressing their political and social views, and their vision for the future. They bring fashion to the level of fine art by using innovative technologies, non-traditional fabrics, silhouettes and garment proportions, as well as using deconstruction/reconstruction methods to develop their collections.

Comme des Garçons	Issey Miyake
Junya Watanabe	Martin Margiela
Hussein Chalayan	Viktor & Rolf
Yohji Yamamoto	Vivienne Westwood

Deconstructed outfit with mixed proportions by Comme des Garçons, Spring/Summer 2008

The Lifestyle Mavens

Lifestyle mavens focus on the well-groomed, high-end customer. They find their inspiration in classic clothing from the the 20s, 30s and 40s, and often refer to the equestrian and bespoke styles from earlier decades. The mavens always start with a classic silhouette, tweak details and adapt traditional design to modern times. Luxury and status are important components of their design philosophy. They use high-quality materials with timeless patterns and finishes that appeal to the eye and are easy to wear. Their collections often include many staple items – a classic tweed jacket, cashmere turtleneck, fair isle sweater vest, pinstripe pants, and a leather satchel – which need no adaptation and are literally ready-to-wear and will be cherished by the customer for life.

Ralph Lauren	Fendi
Michael Kors	Armani
Celine	Gucci
Hermés	Tommy Hilfiger

These are just examples of well-recognised design identities. There are many approaches in modern fashion and each designer chooses their own individual creative path.

Classic, luxury plaids by Michael Kors, Autumn/Winter 2012/13

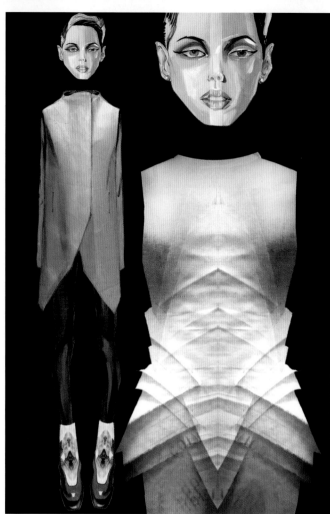

THEORY AND CONCEPT

Perception is reality, shaped by what we know or what we believe. These speculations ensure our survival, but at the same time impede our tolerance and creativity. This collection is a conviction of the multi-faceted nature of reality, and the preconcieved human perception of it. Holographic prints, usually not applied to clothing, are introduced to display multiple images on a single flat surface, brought to life through the movement of the wearer. Therefore, our presumption of seeing a single still image on a textile surface is challenged.

In the design process, a unique photograph of drapings was digitally multiplied and layered, creating a complex structure out of a simple origin.

Digitally multiplied and layered effect.

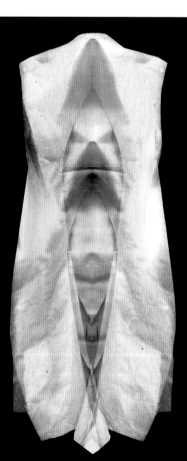

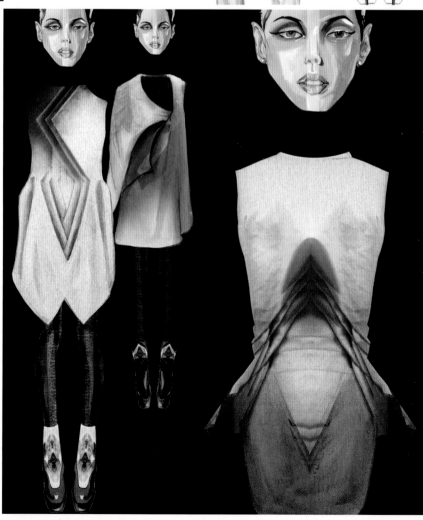

This process of mystification is applied on every garment. In actualising the concept from the digital image, careful design choices were made. The combination of layered fabric creates a multitude of shapes and shades of colours. At first glance, one cannot discern exactly how complicated the structure of each piece is, however, at closer inspection, more and more is discovered.

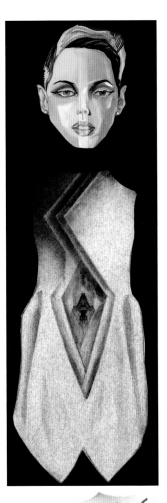

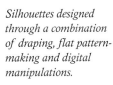

Silhouettes designed through a combination of draping, flat pattern-making and digital manipulations.

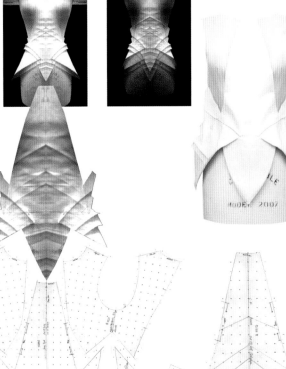

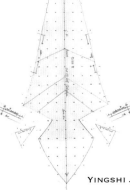

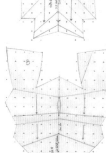

YINGSHI JUNE LIN

DETAILS AND FINISHES

This collection is inspired by the sleek and clean-finished silhouettes of luxury cars and their leather interiors. The collection's main use of pristine nubuck leather, with its smooth and matte surface, give the chic designs a sporty and balanced vibe.

Modern beauty was consistantly used throughout the collection.

Leather colour-blocked helmets, motorcycle gloves and molded snake skin clutches are the perfect accessories.

SCARLET JANG

This sportswear collection revolves around the treatments and techniques that define a luxury car. Stitching, piping, cording, padding and contrasting insert details are the focus and main elements in creating a beautiful structure, while adding sleek finishes to the garment.

A carefully merchandised collection presents a variety of items in many proportions.

corded embosed

snake-skin

leather.

cording

knitted. jacket

Reversed piping

Nubuck patched coat

leggings

leather

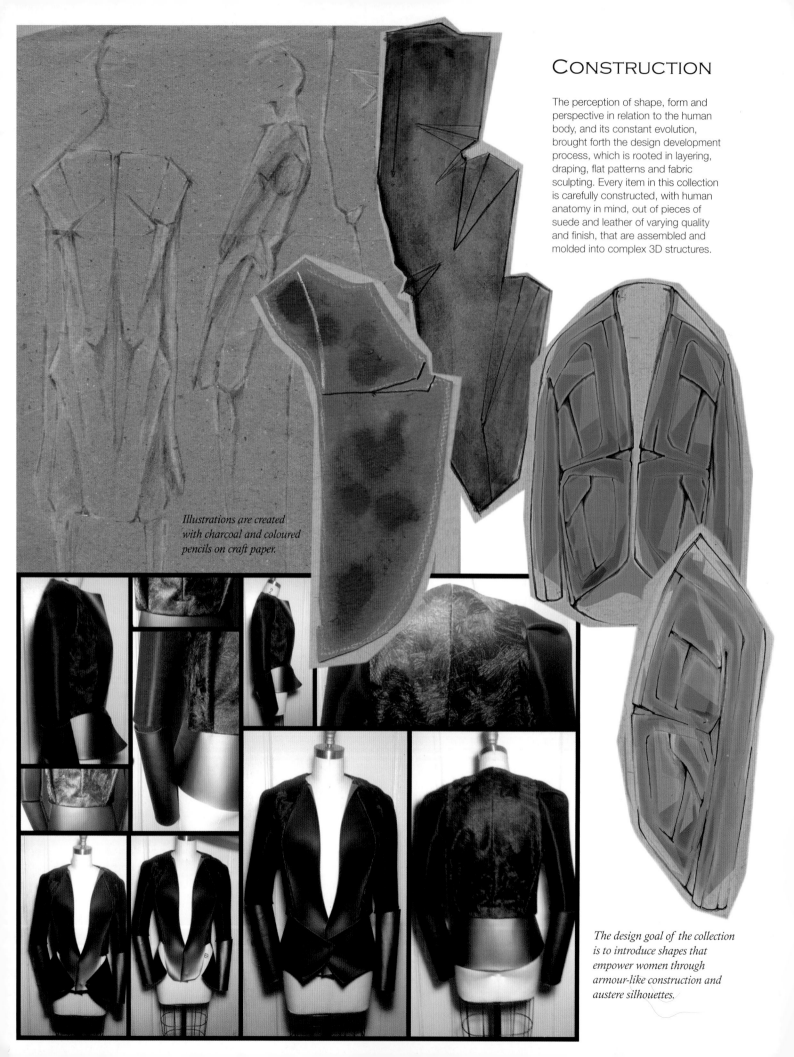

CONSTRUCTION

The perception of shape, form and perspective in relation to the human body, and its constant evolution, brought forth the design development process, which is rooted in layering, draping, flat patterns and fabric sculpting. Every item in this collection is carefully constructed, with human anatomy in mind, out of pieces of suede and leather of varying quality and finish, that are assembled and molded into complex 3D structures.

Illustrations are created with charcoal and coloured pencils on craft paper.

The design goal of the collection is to introduce shapes that empower women through armour-like construction and austere silhouettes.

Stitched and molded leather

VISUAL PERCEPTION

STRUCTURE

JOSHUA MYRIE

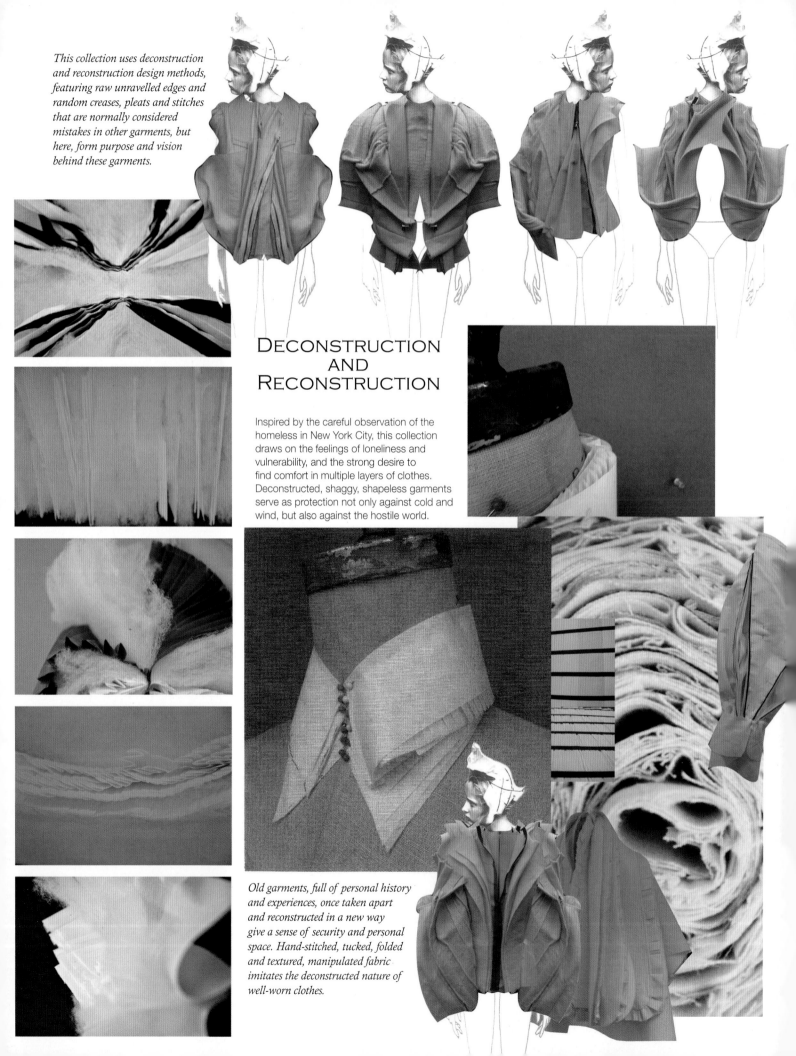

This collection uses deconstruction and reconstruction design methods, featuring raw unravelled edges and random creases, pleats and stitches that are normally considered mistakes in other garments, but here, form purpose and vision behind these garments.

DECONSTRUCTION AND RECONSTRUCTION

Inspired by the careful observation of the homeless in New York City, this collection draws on the feelings of loneliness and vulnerability, and the strong desire to find comfort in multiple layers of clothes. Deconstructed, shaggy, shapeless garments serve as protection not only against cold and wind, but also against the hostile world.

Old garments, full of personal history and experiences, once taken apart and reconstructed in a new way give a sense of security and personal space. Hand-stitched, tucked, folded and textured, manipulated fabric imitates the deconstructed nature of well-worn clothes.

Draping and fabric manipulation stages were digitally photomontaged over a simple figure, creating a distinct rugged-beauty look. Diverse pleats are sculpted into shifts, shrugs and cocoons.

JIE LI

63

Ancient cultures are a rich source for design inspiration and research. Ceremonial masks are an essential element in traditional African culture, and are widely used in ritual dances and events because of their spiritual significance.

ANNA KIPER

CULTURE AND TRADITION

Freehand spontaneous design sketches are juxtaposed with a few final looks, illustrated as flats and executed in marker.

The rustic textures, deep colours, and graphic symmetry of the hand-carved lines of the African masks inspired this contemporary collection. Raw chunky knits, cutout coats, boldly seamed skirts, and dip-dyed dresses are all heavily embellished with hammered-metal beads.

The fabrics are natural fibres, washed, sun-bleached and gently reconstructed.

The concept of surviving a natural disaster or any devastating event is the basis of the design concept and made the collection feel more relevant and necessary, transpiring beyond the idea of an eco project.

A subdued, natural colour palette and austere static figures superimposed over a bleeding watercolour background create a mesmerising atmosphere filled with tranquility and lightness.

MARY SYMCZAK

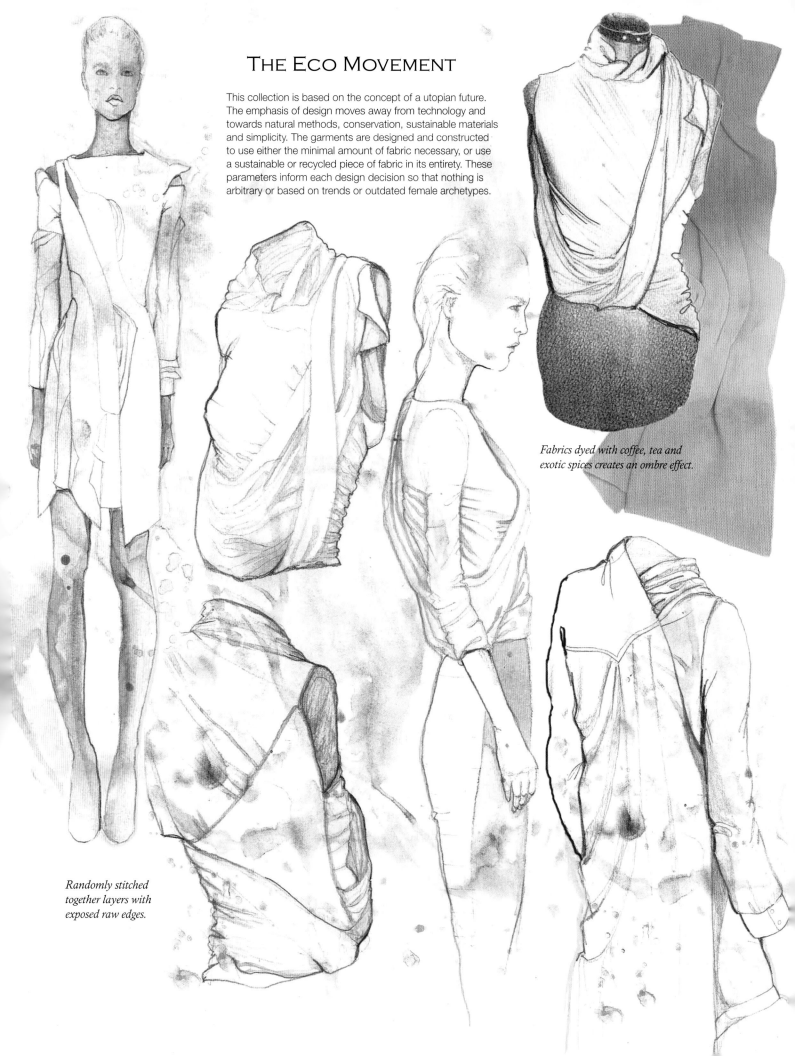

THE ECO MOVEMENT

This collection is based on the concept of a utopian future. The emphasis of design moves away from technology and towards natural methods, conservation, sustainable materials and simplicity. The garments are designed and constructed to use either the minimal amount of fabric necessary, or use a sustainable or recycled piece of fabric in its entirety. These parameters inform each design decision so that nothing is arbitrary or based on trends or outdated female archetypes.

Fabrics dyed with coffee, tea and exotic spices creates an ombre effect.

Randomly stitched together layers with exposed raw edges.

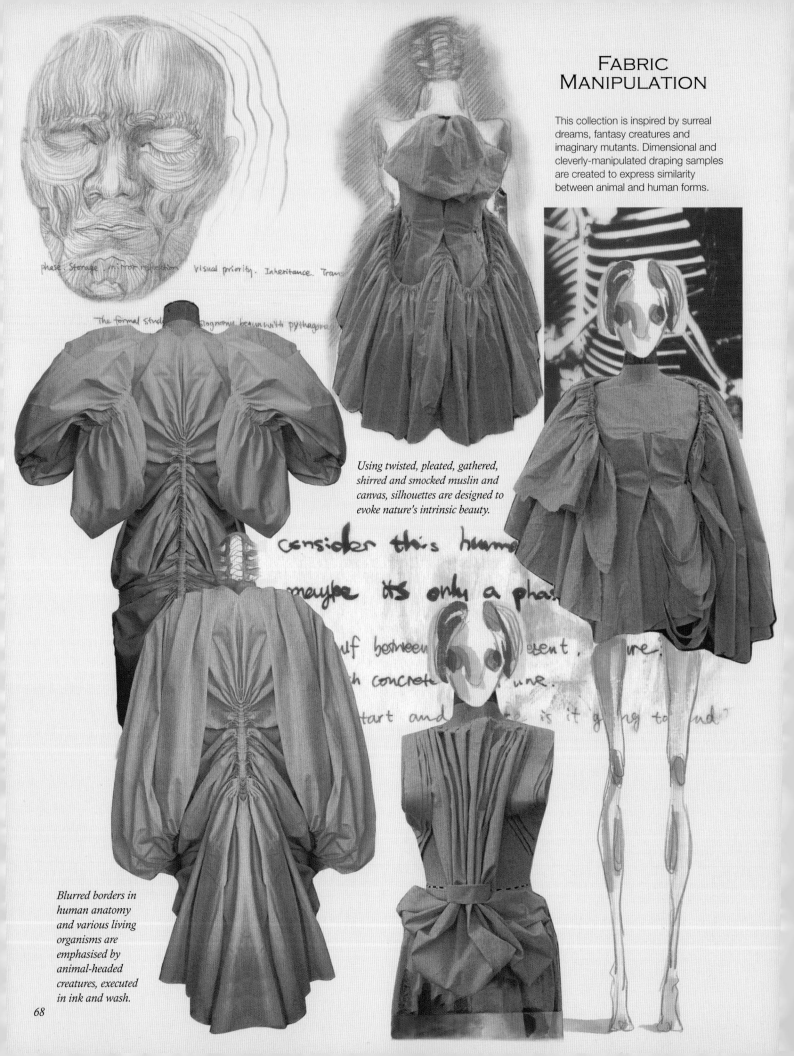

FABRIC MANIPULATION

This collection is inspired by surreal dreams, fantasy creatures and imaginary mutants. Dimensional and cleverly-manipulated draping samples are created to express similarity between animal and human forms.

Using twisted, pleated, gathered, shirred and smocked muslin and canvas, silhouettes are designed to evoke nature's intrinsic beauty.

Blurred borders in human anatomy and various living organisms are emphasised by animal-headed creatures, executed in ink and wash.

By gradually layering strips of muslin and cotton canvas through methodical symmetry, with spontaneous bursts of asymmetry, complex drapings transpired through several design stages.

A macabre mood and monochromatic colour palette enhance the structural quality of the garments.

QUINN ZHU

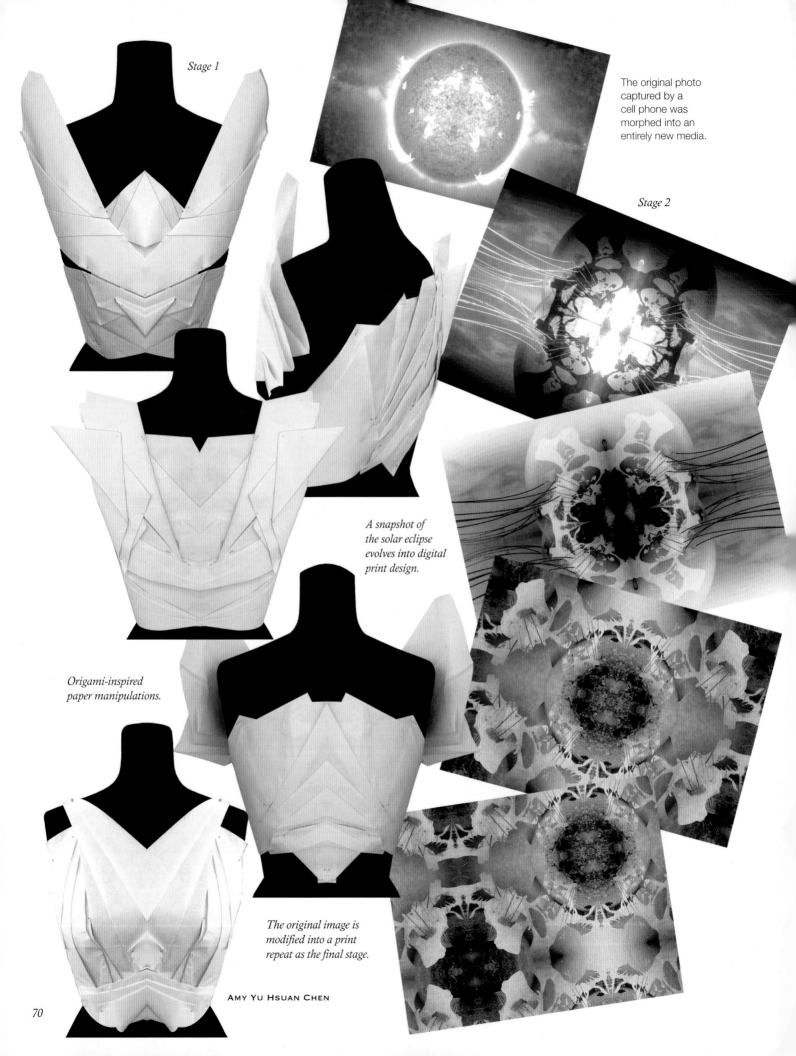

Stage 1

The original photo captured by a cell phone was morphed into an entirely new media.

Stage 2

A snapshot of the solar eclipse evolves into digital print design.

Origami-inspired paper manipulations.

The original image is modified into a print repeat as the final stage.

AMY YU HSUAN CHEN

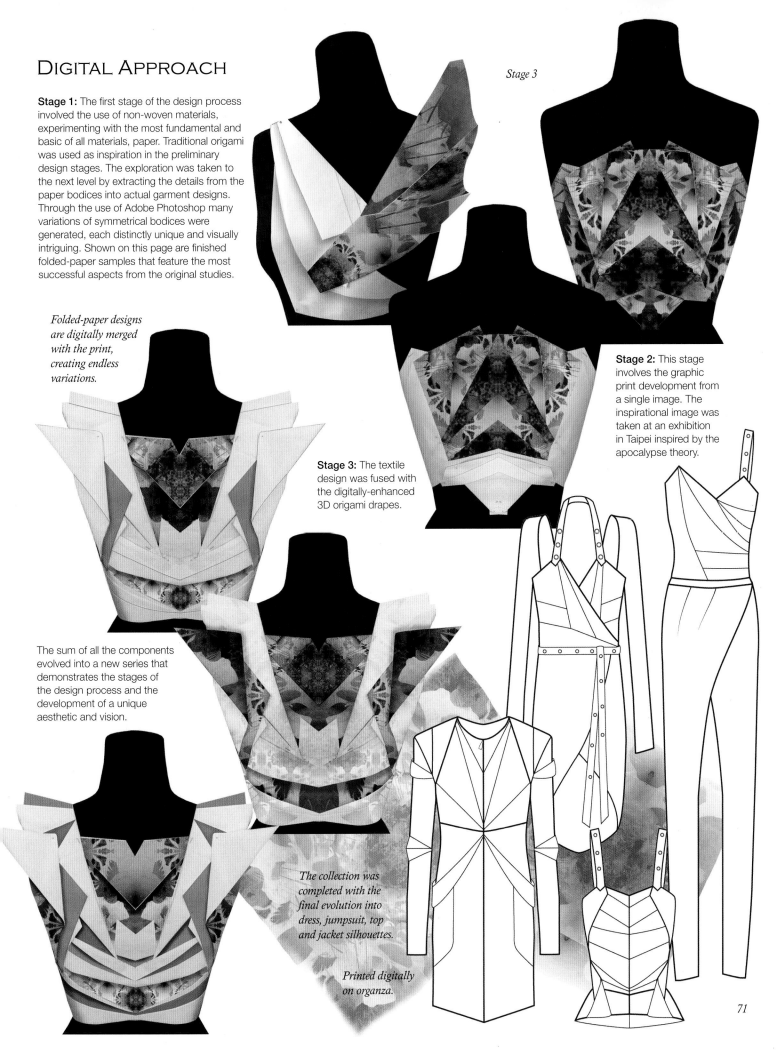

DIGITAL APPROACH

Stage 1: The first stage of the design process involved the use of non-woven materials, experimenting with the most fundamental and basic of all materials, paper. Traditional origami was used as inspiration in the preliminary design stages. The exploration was taken to the next level by extracting the details from the paper bodices into actual garment designs. Through the use of Adobe Photoshop many variations of symmetrical bodices were generated, each distinctly unique and visually intriguing. Shown on this page are finished folded-paper samples that feature the most successful aspects from the original studies.

Folded-paper designs are digitally merged with the print, creating endless variations.

Stage 3

Stage 2: This stage involves the graphic print development from a single image. The inspirational image was taken at an exhibition in Taipei inspired by the apocalypse theory.

Stage 3: The textile design was fused with the digitally-enhanced 3D origami drapes.

The sum of all the components evolved into a new series that demonstrates the stages of the design process and the development of a unique aesthetic and vision.

The collection was completed with the final evolution into dress, jumpsuit, top and jacket silhouettes.

Printed digitally on organza.

PRESENTATION TECHNIQUES

Presentation style should convey one's personal aesthetic, support the overall design concept, and tell a story about the collection. Strong attention to details, such as colour, fabrics, image selection, illustration styles and media, will help communicate intent and the unique aspects of the design. Originality and experimentation with materials and formats will create a memorable, impactful and unpredictable portfolio of work that reflects a signature style.

COLOUR

It is important for a designer to have a good eye for harmonious colour combinations, understanding that basic colour theory is essential for contemporary palette development and colour mixing.

The colour wheel is a simplified version of the rainbow spectrum.

Primary Colours *red, blue and yellow, cannot be created by mixing other colours.*

Secondary Colours *orange, green and violet, are formed by mixing two primary colours.*

YG

BG

BV

RV

RO

YO

Analogous Colours *like orange, red-orange and red have a common hue and are positioned next to each other on the colour wheel.*

Complimentary Colours *are the direct opposites on the colour wheel, for example red and green. Mixing two complementary colours always results in a dark neutral or a shade of grey.*

Tertiary Colours *are produced by mixing a primary and a secondary colour, for example mixing blue with green, creating a blue-green.*

Saturation *is the density of colour.*

Tints *are created by adding white to a colour.*

Shades *are formed by adding measured amounts of black to the colour.*

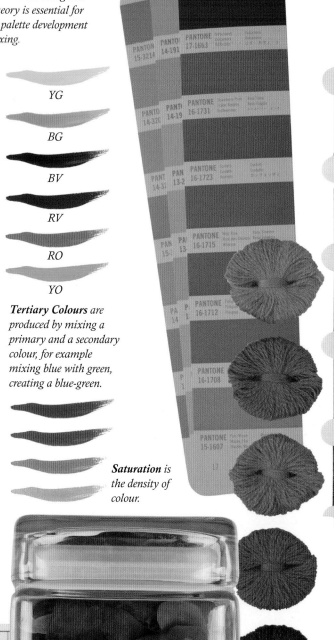

Fabric swatches and yarns as colour references.

Value is the amount of lightness and darkness in a colour. *Tone* indicates the level of shade or tint in a colour. *Hue* is the gradations and variations of a colour.

In the process of looking for points of inspiration, colour research becomes one of the fundamental elements of the design process. Since colour can evoke emotional responses, the mood of a collection is subconsciously associated with a specific colour scheme. Washed-out pastels recall the soft and dreamy atmosphere of a snowy winter; on the contrary, jewel tones are commonly associated with high glamour, power and wealth.

Using colours assocated with everyday items (e.g. elements, stones, spices and plants), colours are often named in reference to these, such as charcoal grey, ice blue, emerald green, paprika red, lilac or lavender.

Inspired by the refined colour sense of well-known artists, designers frequently base their seasonal palettes on works of famous colourists like Matisse or Paul Klee. While creating a palette, aside from colour chips and yarns, materials like ribbons, fabric swatches, paints, pastels and even small glass tiles are creatively used as colour references. The best way of indicating an exact tone of a particular colour is to use a standardised colour-matching system; for example Pantone, contains nearly 2,000 chromatically organised colour chips.

73

FABRIC PRESENTATION

Fabrics, presented artistically, following the design aesthetic of the collection, will create a significant visual impact.

Swatches stitched to metal mesh

Textiles board inspired by spices

Fabrics set in frames

Neatly trimmed or left with fraying edges, fabrics should be organised in harmony to convey the mood of the collection. Leaving textiles exposed for touch will add an interactive element to a portfolio, engaging the viewer.

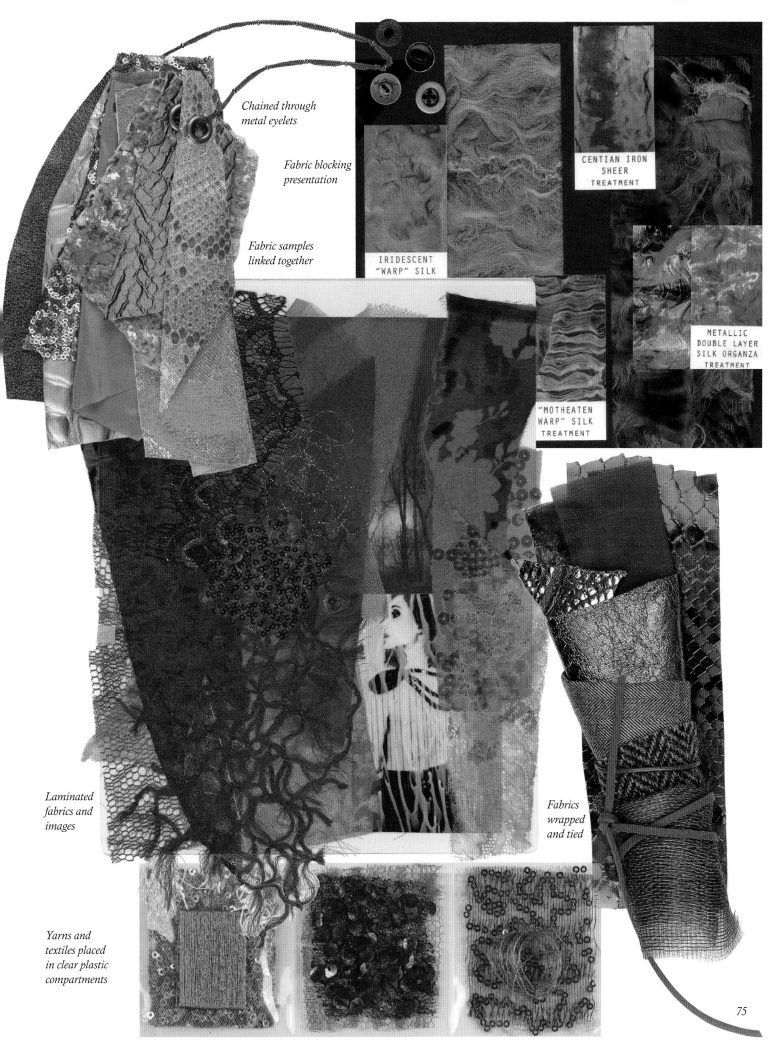

Chained through
metal eyelets

Fabric blocking
presentation

Fabric samples
linked together

Laminated
fabrics and
images

Yarns and
textiles placed
in clear plastic
compartments

IRIDESCENT
"WARP" SILK

CENTIAN IRON
SHEER
TREATMENT

METALLIC
DOUBLE LAYER
SILK ORGANZA
TREATMENT

"MOTHEATEN
WARP" SILK
TREATMENT

Fabrics
wrapped
and tied

layered and
appliquéd

screen printed
and beaded

patchwork

ropes and
lace

cut felt

stones and chains

vegetable dyes

folded and braided
leather strips

Designers frequently create unique
textile samples experimenting
with various approaches and
techniques in order to test new
ideas and develop prototypes.
In the small format of a swatch
it is easier to test innovative
methods and materials, as well as
unexpected textile combinations.

clear tubes
and yarns

wire, beads
and plaster

heat-melted angelina fibre

fused tulle,
lace and sequins

gel cords
and paillettes

heat-melted angelina fibre

felted yarns

screen printed

Similar to garment collections, textile developments are often created with themes in mind. Experimenting with different materials and techniques or exploring a single media, a textile collection should have a cohesive colour pallet and mood.

dip-dyed and beaded

hand knitted

stencil transfer

These samples are designed to resemble elements in nature, in particular the textural surface of tree bark and the organic silhouettes of branches. Any inspiration can be conceptualised to create more abstract outcomes.

digitally printed

felted

This collection of surface design samples is inspired by the fascinating sea creature, the octopus. Hand-painted swatches resemble the shape of this dynamic monster/animal and the trails of ink it leaves behind.

Hand-painted textiles on this page by Victoria Hayes.

These textiles are developed using fabric paints, ink, acrylic, and paint pens applied to duchess satin, charmeuse and silk organza. Since fabrics tend to absorb most paint pigments, several coats of paint are applied to achieve the desired opacity of colour. Chiffon and fine jersey respond well to dip-dyeing and soaking in inks.

original image

IMAGE MANIPULATION

Beautiful and expressive images are a crucial element of the design presentation. They bring to life fabric and story boards, pages of the design journal or a portfolio, placed aside sketches for mood and colour references. It's always best to use original photography, but it is also possible to manipulate existing images, adapting them to the specific mood and colour story.

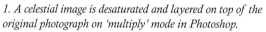

1. A celestial image is desaturated and layered on top of the original photograph on 'multiply' mode in Photoshop.
2. The photograph is copied, flipped and layered on multiply mode. The reticulation filter adds grain and desired colours.
3. The photograph is copied and layered at 50% opacity with inverted values.
4. Splashes of paint are scanned and layered on top of the original photograph on multiply mode.

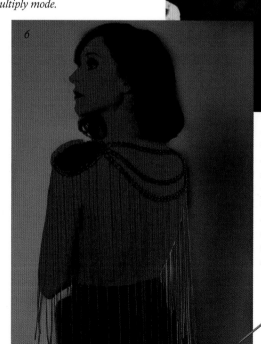

5. Image copied on clear acetate and superimposed over an abstract floral collage.
6. Areas are selected using the lasso tool. Hue and saturation are manipulated differently for each selection.

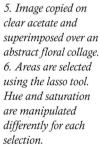

80

7. The effect is created by dripping white nail polish on vellum paper print.

8. Inverted colour mode of previous image, with adjusted level of contrast.

9. Chemically transferred image to a strip of clear film, edges taped with red acetate strips.

10. Cut out in Photoshop with background changed to sepia, the image is overlaid on an abstract artwork.

11. After changing the contrast of the original image in Photoshop, and placing another artwork over it, the overlay settings were adjusted.

12. Blue bleeding into black, the gradient effect was applied to the background in Photoshop and overlaid with a scanned lace detail.

13. Image printed on watercolour paper, loosely painted and collaged with cut-out pieces of black lace.

14. Blue and magenta acetate prints of the original image inverted and layered with a slight shift over a painted background.

MOOD AND PRESENTATION

Drssing while asleep
subconscious freedom of
unconstructed clothes...
...in a senseless way

Mood is one of the most essential
components of design development.
Closely related to inspiration and a
collection's purpose, mood can be
expressed through many elements.
While crafting a presentation, designers
relate beautiful, carefully selected
images to colour palettes, yarns,
textiles and trims to create a desired
mood. From choice of paper, to
illustration style and media, every visual
element evokes the envisioned mood
and artistic feeling of the collection.

*This knitwear story, inspired by a sense of sleep, illuminates a serene
mood of light dreaming mixed with vague sounds from outside, making
it impossible to separate reality from fantasy. Dark, surreal images with
subdued colours and bleeding edges underline the emotional aspect of the
theme, bringing out relevant associations and memories. Complex weaving
and knitting systems with floating textured yarns, hanging threads and
bulky twisted cables are expressed with tone-on-tone bleeding ink.*

- Midnight silver
- Salutary whites
- Calming creams
- Hypnotic metalics
- Mesmerizing blues
- Grey dusk
- Faded umber

You are wrapped, draped and folded in dreams....
Dreams are fused with your mind and body...
...Dream...

A mood of serenity, calm harmony and tranquility...
....Dreams and desires have no boundaries, they inspire new possibilities...

ANNA KIPER

Mood boards set the atmosphere and energy of the future collection, serving as a prelude to design development.

83

FINAL PRESENTATION

Design ideas are commonly expressed through visuals – sketch books and journals, mood, colour and fabric boards, as well as illustrations.

inspiration and mood

creative journal

The hand-crafted inspiration journal portrays the beauty and complexity of the world by layering transparent, acetate images over the intricate base images.

textile and yarn samples

fabric and trim board

colour story

White, icy blue and crisp mint fabrics include ombre-dyed knits, felting and brocade. Static, modern illustrations look faded and surreal, magically peeking through snow or fog.

design sketches

This collection is inspired by the tragic life and death of the legendary Korean Dynasty Empress Min. The royal empress represents the contrasting qualities of vulnerability and strength, in a time that was both calm and chaotic.

Her existence was like a snowflake, complex and perfect like the colour white, which reflects and radiates all other colours.

CLAUDIA BAIK

85

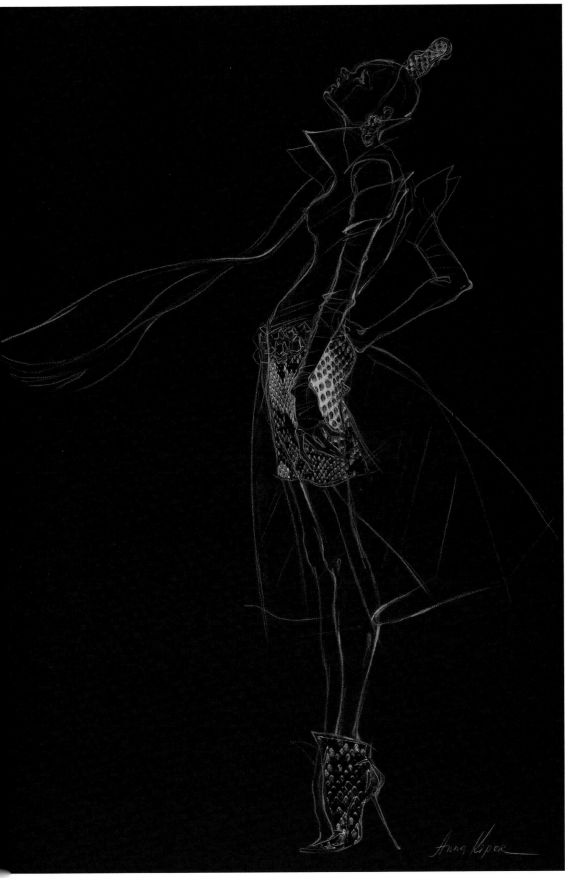

Recently recognised as a contemporary art form, fashion illustration is a vital element in the design process. From rough design journal sketches, diagrams and technical flats to fully finished mood illustrations, fashion drawing is a unique expression of the designer's personal style. For many designers drawing serves as a strong visual language and an effective way of translating and sharing their ideas. While presenting ideas in sketches, designers communicate their aesthetic and design sensibility though specific illustration styles and media. Charged with creative energy, original and expressive illustrations will personalise any portfolio leaving a strong impression on the viewer.

A unique and original illustration style emerges from life experiences, exposure to cultures and art, endless drawing practices and media experimentations. Closely observing trends in society and fashion, designers should reflect these ideas in their work.

In developing personal style, the following points should be addressed:

Choice of Media: Watercolour, markers, gouache, ink, collage, digital and mixed media.

Illustration Style: Realistic, stylised, abstract, minimalistic.

Figure Drawing Approach: Simplistic, static or exaggerated dynamic poses.

Rendering Style: Simplified partial, artistic spontaneous mixed media, dimensional, detailed and realistic rendering.

It is important to keep in mind that some media requires specific paper selection. For example, the sharpness and depth of watercolour renderings often depend on the weight, texture and quality of watercolour paper. As well, markers behave differently on various brands of marker paper, vellum or sheer tracing.

ANNA KIPER

White pencil on black paper illustrations, with collage placed strategically to reinforce the flow on the page.

Media and Supplies

1. *Eye shadows*

2. *Ink and dyes*

3. *Watercolour*

4. *Gouache*

5. *Brush pens*

6. *Copic markers*

7. *Tria markers*

8. *Prismacolor markers*

9. *Chartpack markers*

10. *Watercolour pencils*

11. *Le Pen*

12. *Prismacolor pencils*

13. *Verithin pencils*

14. *Metallic pens*

15. *Coloured pens*

16. *Pastels*

17. *Paint markers*

18. *Bamboo reed pens*

19. *Brushes*

20. *X-Acto knife*

Media is a defining element of any presentation. Affecting the look and style of the illustrations, media should be selected with consideration of the specific project and skill level of the artist. The choice of media could have a dramatic visual impact on the drawing. For example, watercolour is transparent with bleeding edges, gouache is flat and opaque, and pastel is textured. Enhancing the design aspect of the presentation, the chosen media should closely reflect the mood and aesthetic of the illustrated collection.

The overwhelming selection of art supplies is offered in many brands and at a range of price points. For any media, sampling and exploring creative materials is the best way to choose the right tools for the project.

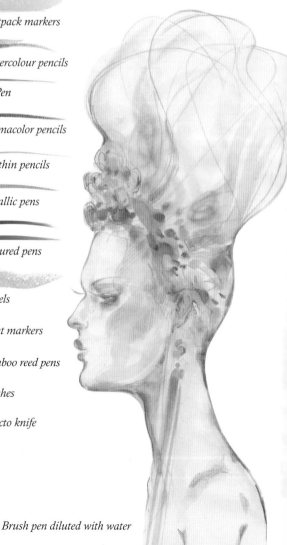

Brush pen diluted with water

Watercolour and watercolour pencils

Markers and eye shadows

Each media requires a specific choice of paper and, unfortunately, all-purpose paper often fails to perform for many media. For example, watercolour requires watercolour paper, but the specific weight and quality should be selected through testing and experiments. Markers dry out quickly if applied on anything besides marker paper. They don't work at all on craft paper, which on the contrary, is perfectly suitable for pastels, coloured pencils and even brush pens.

Gouache on coloured paper

Coloured pencils and pastels on craft paper

ANNA KIPER

1. Freehand silhouettes of figures are gently sketched on marker paper with a light tone marker. Any imperfections in the initial drawing will be camouflaged by the subsequent marker layers.

2. Base colours are applied loosely and partially to create the background for future textures and prints. The facial features start to emerge with the light touches of a brush-tip marker.

3. Shading is created in several tonal layers. Each layer is slightly darker and deeper then the previous and should be carefully blended around the edges.

4. Details are brought out and prints are filled in with a fine-tip marker. Accessories and beauty are accented with bolder smudges of colour.

MARKER RENDERING

Markers are one of the most popular illustration tools. All brands and types of markers mix easily with coloured pencils and ink pens, which can be used for prints, textures and outlines. Multi-dimensional and vibrant artworks can be achieved by gradual application of marker layers, followed by the softening of edges around each layer with a clear blender marker. The effect can be compared to the bleeding and transparent nature of watercolour.

Markers are usually applied over a detailed pencil sketch. Sometimes to avoid pencil smudges the sketch can be placed underneath semi-transparent marker paper and after the colours are applied the original drawing should be carefully traced to the top page. Some marker rendering techniques are achieved without a preliminary pencil drawing. In that case the initial sketch is created directly with markers, and the pencil outline becomes the last step.

5. A contrasting coloured pencil outline becomes the last step of the process. Stronger at times or fading and even disappearing, the outline should be effortless and organic, to create a beautiful line quality.

ANNA KIPER

1. Light pencil drawings created on craft paper consider the figure's flow and movement. Small details and motifs for future prints are applied.

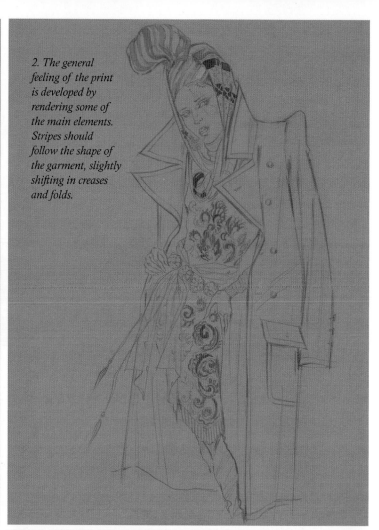

2. The general feeling of the print is developed by rendering some of the main elements. Stripes should follow the shape of the garment, slightly shifting in creases and folds.

3. To express dimension, shadows and highlights are introduced. Details of the prints are gradually developed.

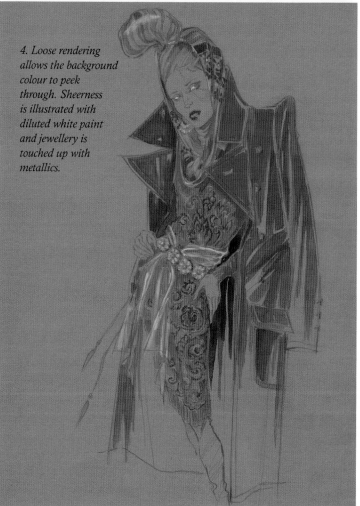

4. Loose rendering allows the background colour to peek through. Sheerness is illustrated with diluted white paint and jewellery is touched up with metallics.

92

GOUACHE RENDERING

Gouache, an opaque, water-based paint, works on vellum, coloured or craft paper. Perfect for textile colour matching, gouache could be mixed in any proportion with water for transparency effects or tinted and shaded with white or black. Light saturated paint tones could be layered over dark grounds – a technique impossible to achieve in marker or watercolour rendering. Gouache mixes well with coloured pencils and ink, and could be applied to paper with flat or rounded brushes, as well as sponges for various textures and effects.

5. Facial features are gently painted leaving skin tone as the natural colour of the background. Stronger shadows, pencil touches and a black bleeding background completes the drawing.

ANNA KIPER

1. An exotic line drawing was created with an indigo-coloured pigma micron pen on a light marker paper. Preliminary pencil lines and marks were erased, and some of the ink outline was thickened for dimension and line quality effects.

2. The ink drawing was scanned and inkjet printed on watercolour paper. Candle wax marks were added to the print for a highlight effect before any contact with paint or water. Generous amounts of water were applied to the drawing prior to painting to create a bleeding effect.

3. Loose layers of paint were premixed into complex shades on the palette before being dropped on a wet paper surface. With every point of contact with the wet paper, the paint runs, bleeds and mixes with other colour stains, creating unpredictable combinations.

4. Gently applied with a wide rounded brush, watercolour dries quickly, becoming several shades lighter. For that reason shadow colours are premixed in darker and deeper tones. Shadows blend organically when applied while the existing layers are still wet.

5. This innovative technique, which includes both digital and manual processes, allows the combination of a sharp ink outline (which is only possible on light marker paper) with the ethereal effects of watercolour paint.

WATERCOLOUR RENDERING

Watercolour is a translucent water-based paint, usually applied over watercolour paper, which comes in a variety of finishes and weights.

Loosely layered, watercolour creates beautiful, accidental bleed marks and stains, while still allowing the textured paper surface to be visible. Watercolour is spontaneous and vibrant, delicate and sheer at the same time, and makes this unique media perfectly suitable for both dramatic evening wear drawings as well as lacy, transparent lingerie sketches.

Generously diluted with water, watercolour often expands, drips and runs beyond the outlines of the drawing, creating magical shapes and textures. Any attempts to reapply paint over the same spot again could damage the tie-dye like effect by leaving flat, opaque stains.

ANNA KIPER

PAGE COMPOSITION

Portfolios created with energy and an emphasis on page composition, always have a stronger impact on the viewer. Various page layout approaches are used depending on the mood, style and format of the presentation. Regardless of which style of composition is used, it should always be planned, not accidental.

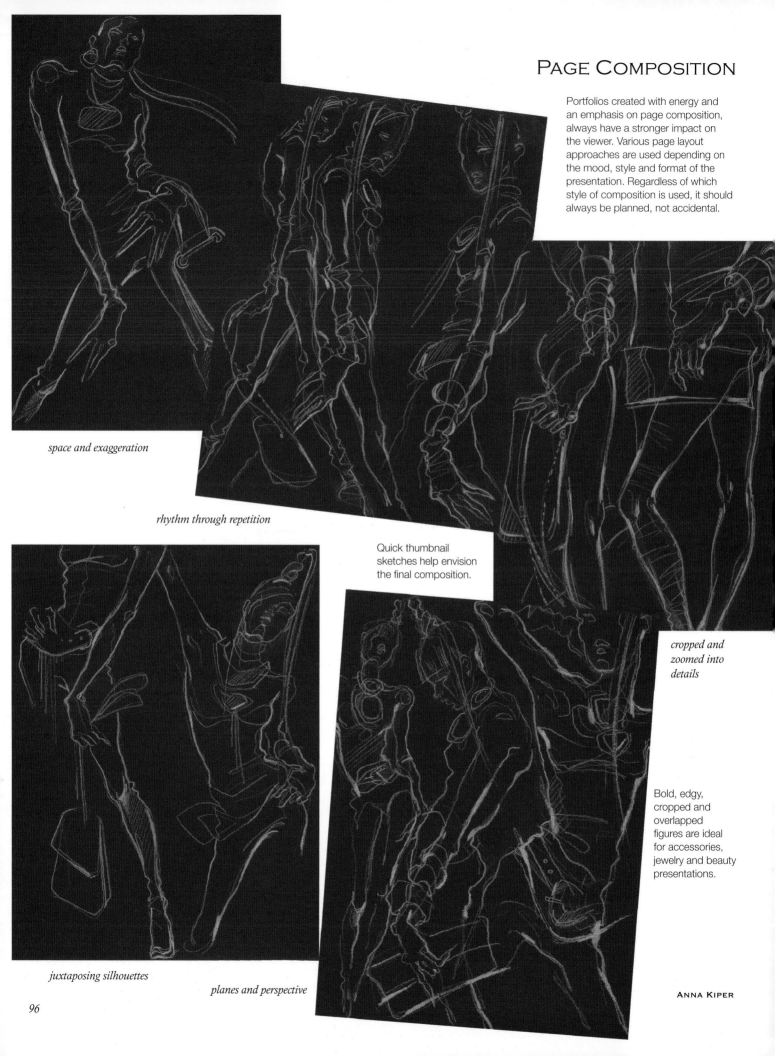

space and exaggeration

rhythm through repetition

Quick thumbnail sketches help envision the final composition.

cropped and zoomed into details

Bold, edgy, cropped and overlapped figures are ideal for accessories, jewelry and beauty presentations.

juxtaposing silhouettes

planes and perspective

ANNA KIPER

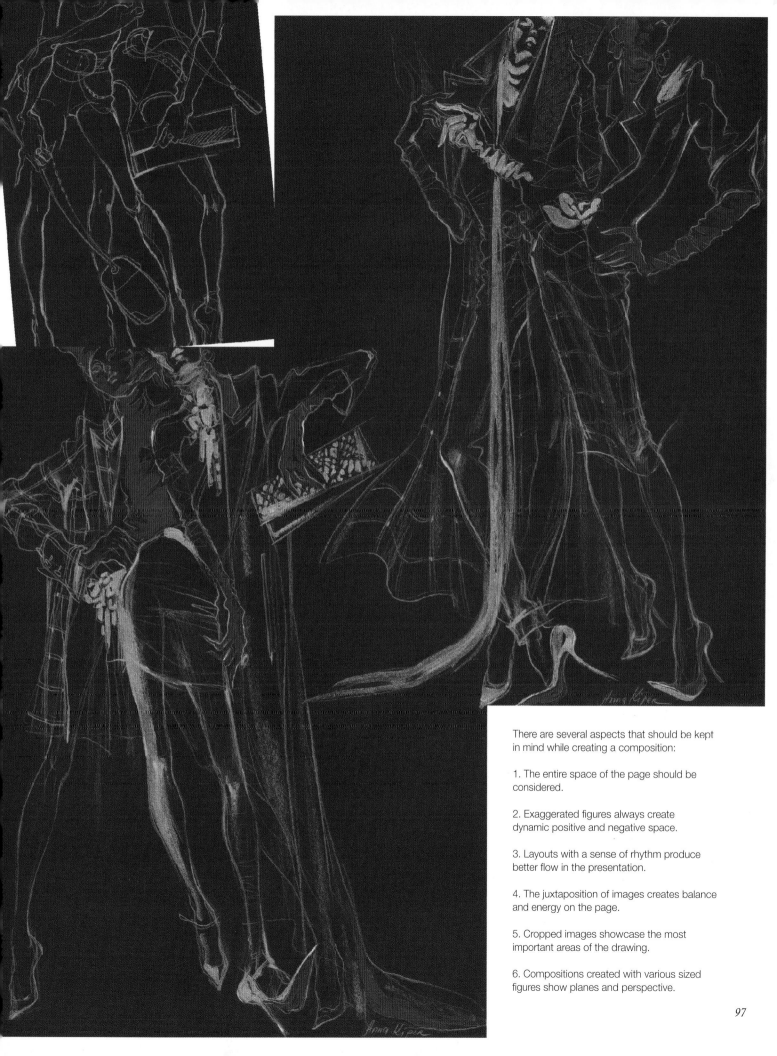

There are several aspects that should be kept in mind while creating a composition:

1. The entire space of the page should be considered.

2. Exaggerated figures always create dynamic positive and negative space.

3. Layouts with a sense of rhythm produce better flow in the presentation.

4. The juxtaposition of images creates balance and energy on the page.

5. Cropped images showcase the most important areas of the drawing.

6. Compositions created with various sized figures show planes and perspective.

ILLUSTRATION STYLES

Black pen, collage.
Animation style.

JIAYU LI

Bleeding ink.
Abstract style.

JAYLIN
YONGCHU
RHEW

Watercolour.
Minimalistic.

HEEWON YANG

An ability to communicate ideas through drawing is essential for designers. Fashion sketches not only allow designers to visualise garment details and proportions, but also to express their individual sensibility and personal style. Unique illustration styles are as valuable as the design content of the portfolio, making it unique and memorable.

Gouache, ink and coloured pencils. Photorealistic style.

LISA LEE

Pencil outline, digitally rendered. Stylised.

ELIN JOHANSSON

Whether watercolour, gouache, ink, collage or marker rendering, any media choice should complement the feel of the specific collection and the designer's creative vision. A figure's attitude, proportions and beauty are crucial elements in the development of the signature illustration style and should closely represent an ideal customer.

Marker, brush pen, and white gouache on craft paper. Exaggerated style.

JIN HWA LEE

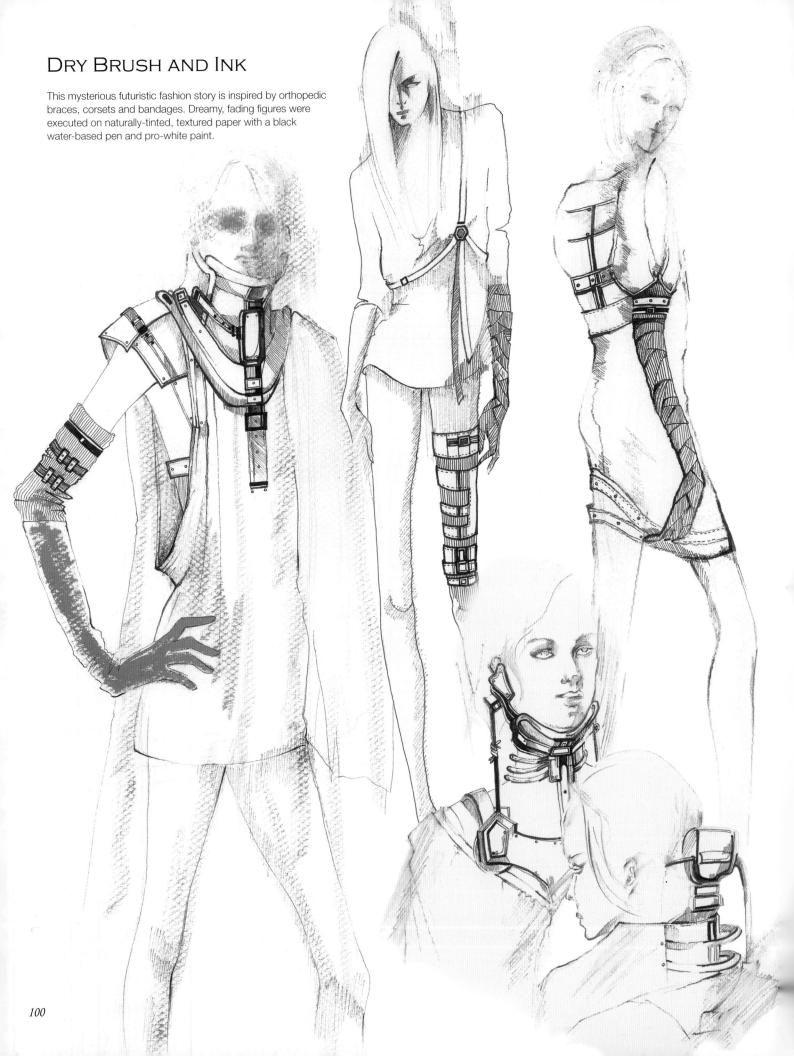

DRY BRUSH AND INK

This mysterious futuristic fashion story is inspired by orthopedic braces, corsets and bandages. Dreamy, fading figures were executed on naturally-tinted, textured paper with a black water-based pen and pro-white paint.

Bodies and faces were executed in a dry brush technique, applying light, neutral colours of paint in layers. Initially, faces were outlined and shaded with black water-based pen applied over a light pencil sketch. Pro-white paint is layered on top with a very small amount of water. Black water-based pen will slightly bleed and mix with the pro-white paint creating a blurry, out-of-focus look.

The intricate elements of the body braces are executed with various black ink pens. High definition linear details superimposed over softly faded figures creates a stunning impact, defining an unforgettable illustration style.

Yoonhee Joe

WATERCOLOUR LAYERS

These illustrations were created in layers, starting with watercolour paint splattered on paper and spread with water and blown with air. Several versions were created and superimposed digitally on shades of grey and beige paper. Using pencil and acrylic paint, figures were sketched and rendered on top of the watercolour background. Finally, illustrations were merged with photocopies of draped fabric, blending all elements into one composition.

It is essential to test design ideas in muslin, comparing the 3D silhouettes to the original drawings, as well as developing new sketches inspired by spontaneous draping. Generated in design journals, this creative approach can also be included in the final presentation.

MARY SYMCZAK

PHOTOMONTAGE

The complex pattern is drawn with India ink, becoming one of the key elements of the collection.

This stunning portfolio spread was created by combining fine ink outlines, soft gouache skin tone renderings and a sophisticated photomontage of beautifully draped fabrics.

The gouache and India ink illustrations, with manually draped and digitally enhanced garments, are meticulously layered on top of the hand-drawn figures.

Colourful and futuristic accessories, along with a simplistic, monochromatic hairstyle, are a perfect counterbalance to the intricate and visually stimulating designs.

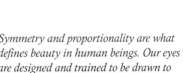

Symmetry and proportionality are what defines beauty in human beings. Our eyes are designed and trained to be drawn to symmetry, but this quality is subtle.

What if this concept could be applied to clothing? This undefinable, yet alluring, theme is echoed in this collection which is based on soft draping and an unstructured silhouette. The poses of the figures are stationary to emphasise the symmetry of the garments, which are presented in layers and can be worn separately. Each layer adds to the complexity of the look, but does not disrupt its coherence.

YINGSHI JUNE LIN

This collection is inspired by the work of contemporary French artist Benjamin Carbonne, who brilliantly expresses human anatomy through the use of energetic, almost violent, brush strokes and an emotionally charged, somber colour palette. This drawing technique is similarly dynamic; a painterly and absolutely ideal illustration style for this stark geometric collection.

PETER DO

GOUACHE AND BRUSH PEN

Executed in gouache and brush pen on craft paper, this bold design story is built from classic pieces with an intense but simple colour story, which includes white, black, shades of brown and splashes of carnal red. Heavily menswear driven, the sharply tailored collection has an androgynous feel emphasised by grotesque, faceless beauty. Colour and fabric blocking combine black, brown and rust highlights creating various modern compositions of layered neoprene, heat-transferred leather, textured knits and fur.

Effortless linear drawings executed in black pen are loosely painted by using gouache with minimal water. The natural craft paper background peeks through layers of paint, and brown brush pen is used to touch up the faces. Partial black backgrounds behind the figures are applied with rough paint smudges, creating a bold graphic effect. The illustrations attract the eye by their spontaneous, austere beauty and artistic yet clear representation of the clothes.

PRESENTATION WITH IMPACT

Every fashion presentation should express the
emotional tone of the collection, closely reflecting
the designer's creative vision and sensibility.

*Fabric selection
creates a rich, jewel-
tone colour story.*

ANNA KIPER

An exotic fantasy collection based on the tales of One Thousand and One Nights.

This imaginative story is told through lush textiles, rustic accessories and expressive illustrations. The transparency of chiffons and the deep richness of velvets are beautifully enhanced by the softness of brushed wools and the shiny reflection of metallic leathers. Sage, tinted gold and spicy brown are highlighted by turquoise, teal and vivid purple colours. Persian and Middle Eastern ornamental jewellery displayed over lavish clothes, suggest an authentic touch and a flavour of far away places.

The loose and fluid illustrations combine mysterious beauty, modern edge and ambiguity. Attention is placed on intriguing facial expressions, profoundly detailed hands and jewellery.

Strongly emphasised hands, slight asymmetry in the face, irregular shading of the eyes and other small touches bring the drawings to life, creating a connection between the artist and viewer, making the illustration memorable.

Snapshots showing how attention to details can create greater impact in the final presentation.

Since the classic portfolio closely resembles a regular book layout, planning the image arrangements as complete spreads is the best way to maintain a seamless flow throughout the presentation. While composing a spread, several points should be addressed – page composition, negative and positive spaces, balance in colour and accents, consistency of styling and beauty.

Bright accents amplified through prints and accessories create rhythm, energy, and consistency throughout the presentation.

Alternating the size of the figures and combining them into clusters by slightly overlapping them will result in a dynamic page composition. Slightly exaggerated poses will create flowing negative spaces between the figures.

ANNA KIPER

Easy, relaxed and mostly frontal poses will allow clear interpretations of the garments, while at the same time giving a modern edge to the presentation.

Silhouettes and fabrications of the outfits should be carefully matched with each figure creating a visual balance of shape, texture and colour on the page.

MOOD AND STYLING

This Shangri-La bohemian design story brings out a slightly different flavour of the exotic East, in comparison to the previous, more refined collection. Addressing the younger customer with a vibrant tapestry of fabrics and casual mismatched ensembles, the collection evokes the 70s Hippie style. Multilingual sounds of the flea markets, the sweet aroma of the spices and tea, old finds, and false treasures inspired an eclectic flats presentation. Handcrafted rustic jewellery and beaded belts are randomly composed over easy and casual clothes.

Loosely rendered freehand mood drawing sets the atmosphere for a vision of colourful, unusual places.

112

Lightly coloured flats styled with collaged ornamental belts and necklaces emphasise the eclectic mood of the collection.

Fair isle, chunky cables, full-fashion knits, slouchy pants, oriental-styled jackets with fur trims and fabric appliqué create a bright patchwork of styles.

ANNA KIPER

113

Opulent freehand figure drawings are executed by layering marker tones and finished with a fine red pencil outline. Realistically rendered textures and bright prints set the colourful vision of oriental exoticism, the land of utopian fantasy and the magical intricacy of ethnic costumes. This presentation format features groups of clustered same-sized figures.

Denims, brocades, printed velvets and ombre knits, corduroys and tweeds are collaged into a fun, off-beat contemporary line. Long fibre fur trims, embroidery, ribbons and fabric inserts, as well as curvy seams and style lines bring out bits and pieces of traditional Tibetan, Mongolian and Russian tunics, vests and coats.

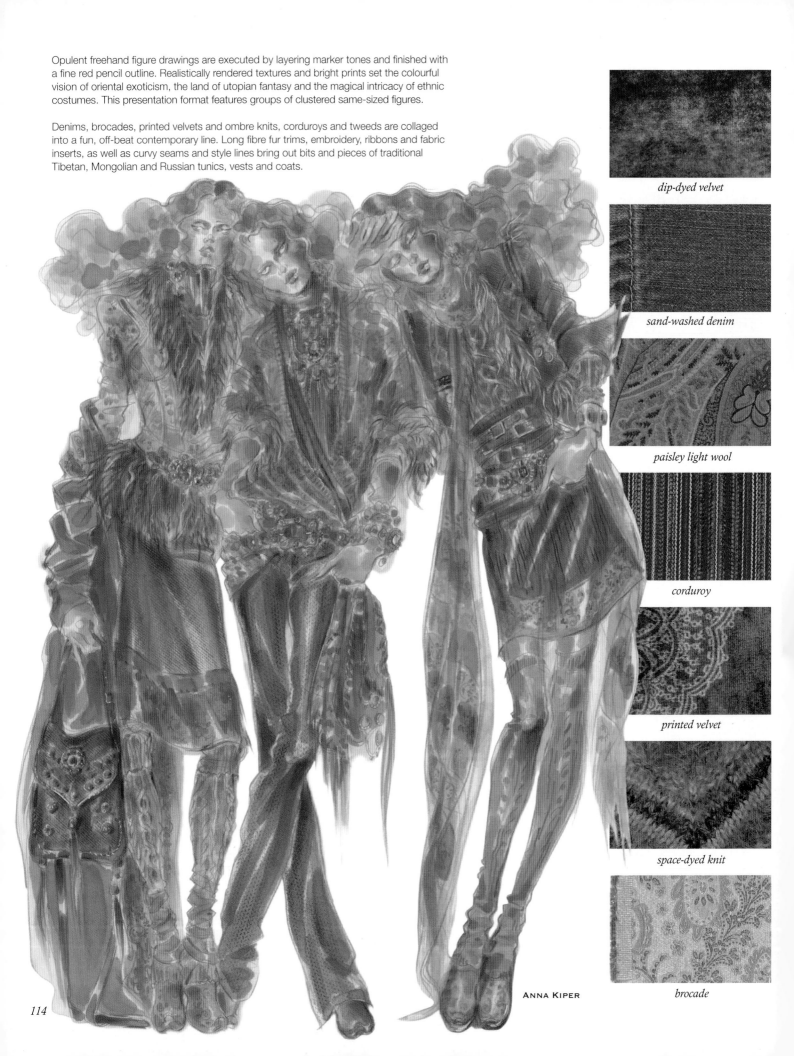

dip-dyed velvet

sand-washed denim

paisley light wool

corduroy

printed velvet

space-dyed knit

brocade

ANNA KIPER

114

From a merchandising standpoint, each textile is used several times in different items for easy mixing and matching. All pieces in a collection are completely interchangeable, and can be combined into a new style with items from other looks, still maintaining the cohesive flow in the collection. Embellished denims and layered knits help to dress down and unify this colourful collection. Folkloric beaded bags, hand-casted ornamental belts and necklaces will work with any look, making styling and merchandising more creative.

cut out

* colour blocked

piping

binding

* all wools

top stitched

double-faced

Mark Rothko's paintings of transcendent fields of mesmerising colour, inspired this fabric-blocked contemporary collection. Collaged, patchworked and stitched fabrics closely resemble the painter's rectangular shapes of brilliant colour, bleeding into the deep darkness of the backgrounds.

Contrasting fabric patching, binding and piping are the essential conceptual elements translating the colour-blocked nature of the paintings.

MODERN ART COLOUR BLOCKING

Faded edges of floating, vibrant strips on the artist's canvases are expressed by raw-edged textured wools and leather layered over tulle, net and sheer nylon. Magenta, coral and cyan blue blurs into beige, black and purple, emulating Rothko's famous colour palettes.

The blocked layout divides the spread into specific sections, allowing focus to fall on each separate part of the presentation: preliminary design sketches, fabric collages, patterns and final figures. Carefully selected media of coloured pencils on craft paper, collage and touches of brush pen support the mood of the collection.

ANNA KIPER

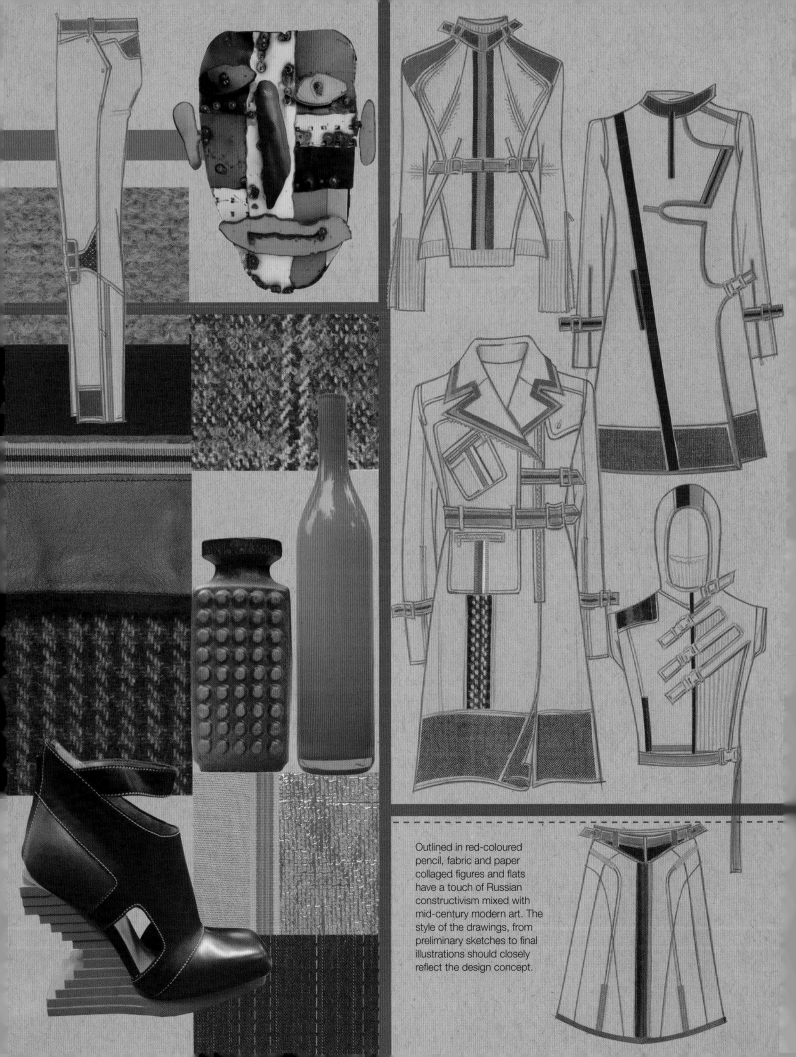

Outlined in red-coloured pencil, fabric and paper collaged figures and flats have a touch of Russian constructivism mixed with mid-century modern art. The style of the drawings, from preliminary sketches to final illustrations should closely reflect the design concept.

From Malevich to Rothko, bold colour and texture blocking always looks impressive in fashion and interior design accessories.

ANNA KIPER

119

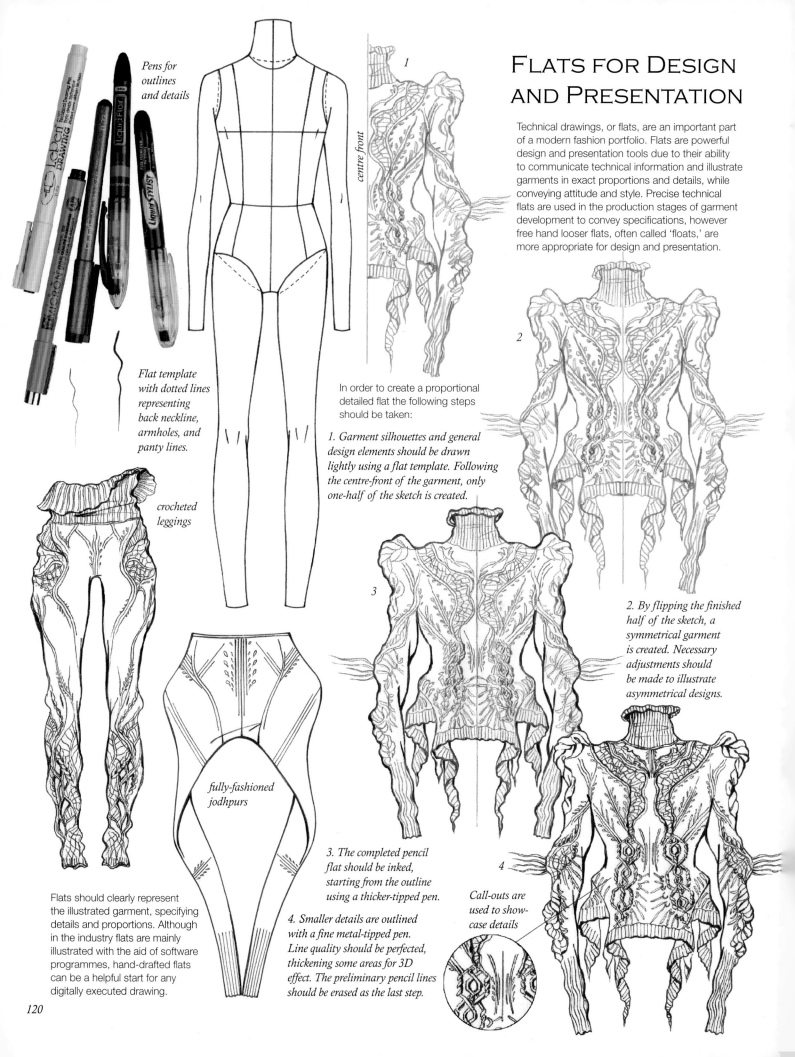

Pens for outlines and details

Flat template with dotted lines representing back neckline, armholes, and panty lines.

centre front

crocheted leggings

fully-fashioned jodhpurs

FLATS FOR DESIGN AND PRESENTATION

Technical drawings, or flats, are an important part of a modern fashion portfolio. Flats are powerful design and presentation tools due to their ability to communicate technical information and illustrate garments in exact proportions and details, while conveying attitude and style. Precise technical flats are used in the production stages of garment development to convey specifications, however free hand looser flats, often called 'floats,' are more appropriate for design and presentation.

In order to create a proportional detailed flat the following steps should be taken:

1. Garment silhouettes and general design elements should be drawn lightly using a flat template. Following the centre-front of the garment, only one-half of the sketch is created.

2. By flipping the finished half of the sketch, a symmetrical garment is created. Necessary adjustments should be made to illustrate asymmetrical designs.

3. The completed pencil flat should be inked, starting from the outline using a thicker-tipped pen.

4. Smaller details are outlined with a fine metal-tipped pen. Line quality should be perfected, thickening some areas for 3D effect. The preliminary pencil lines should be erased as the last step.

Flats should clearly represent the illustrated garment, specifying details and proportions. Although in the industry flats are mainly illustrated with the aid of software programmes, hand-drafted flats can be a helpful start for any digitally executed drawing.

Call-outs are used to show-case details

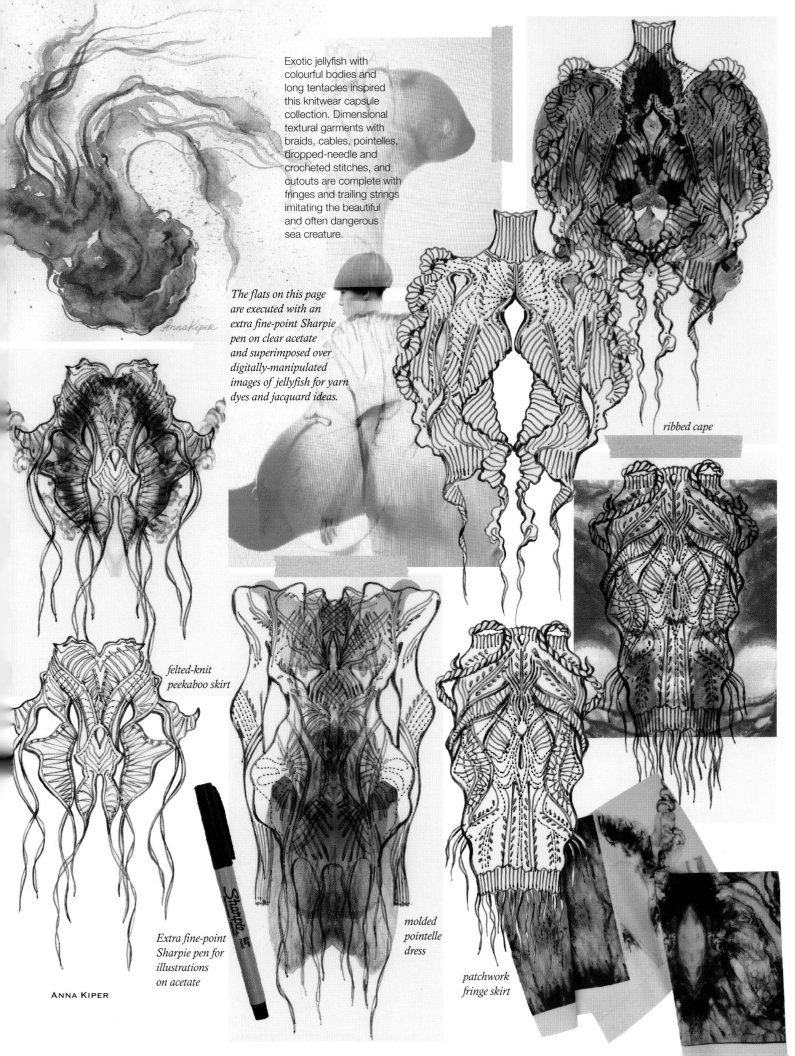

Exotic jellyfish with colourful bodies and long tentacles inspired this knitwear capsule collection. Dimensional textural garments with braids, cables, pointelles, dropped-needle and crocheted stitches, and cutouts are complete with fringes and trailing strings imitating the beautiful and often dangerous sea creature.

The flats on this page are executed with an extra fine-point Sharpie pen on clear acetate and superimposed over digitally-manipulated images of jellyfish for yarn dyes and jacquard ideas.

ribbed cape

felted-knit peekaboo skirt

Extra fine-point Sharpie pen for illustrations on acetate

molded pointelle dress

patchwork fringe skirt

ANNA KIPER

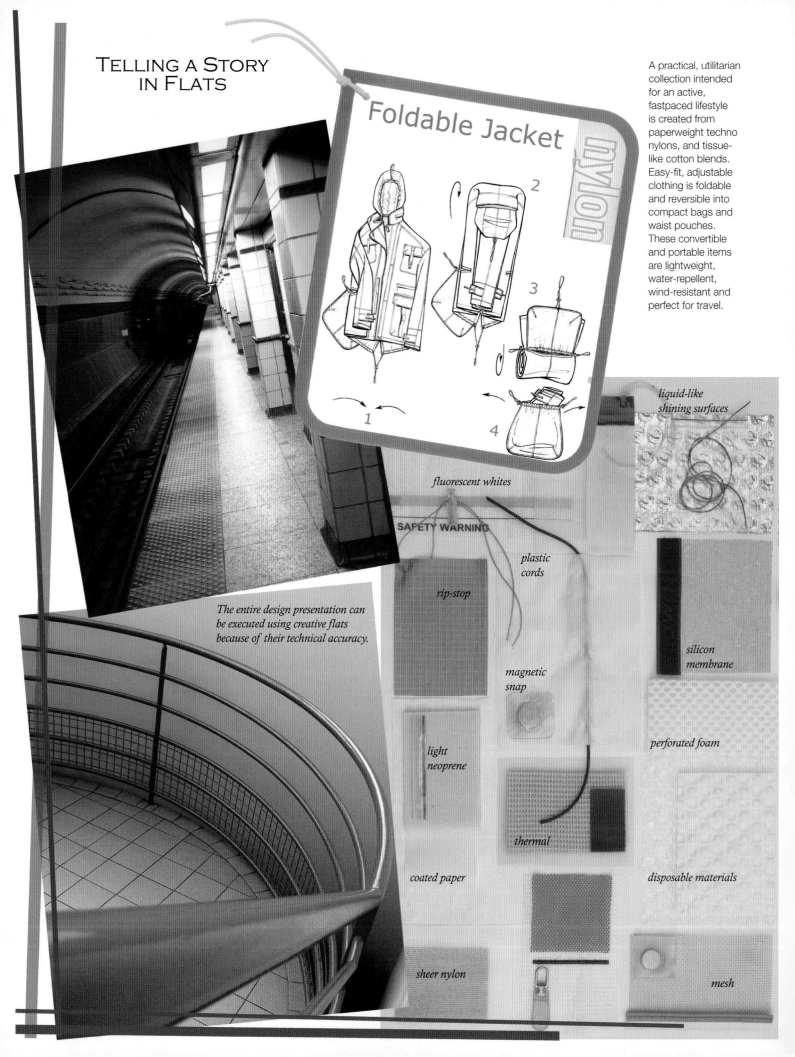

TELLING A STORY IN FLATS

Foldable Jacket

nylon

1 2 3 4

A practical, utilitarian collection intended for an active, fastpaced lifestyle is created from paperweight techno nylons, and tissue-like cotton blends. Easy-fit, adjustable clothing is foldable and reversible into compact bags and waist pouches. These convertible and portable items are lightweight, water-repellent, wind-resistant and perfect for travel.

The entire design presentation can be executed using creative flats because of their technical accuracy.

SAFETY WARNING

fluorescent whites

liquid-like shining surfaces

plastic cords

rip-stop

magnetic snap

silicon membrane

light neoprene

perforated foam

thermal

coated paper

disposable materials

sheer nylon

mesh

Vibrant red drawstring cords, Velcro fastenings and mesh inserts are the bright accents to a white and reflective-silver colour story, peeking through sheer parachute nylons and semi-transparent rip-stops. Strong focus on details, functions and elements are clearly communicated through flat sketches and technical diagrams.

hidden pouch

convertible hood

zip-off belt-bag

clip-on waist adjuster

built-in pouch

sliding compartment

complex pocket system

perforated paper insert

luggage-strap waist band

detachable yoke

key-chain bag

safety buckle

skirt reversible into a pouch

ANNA KIPER

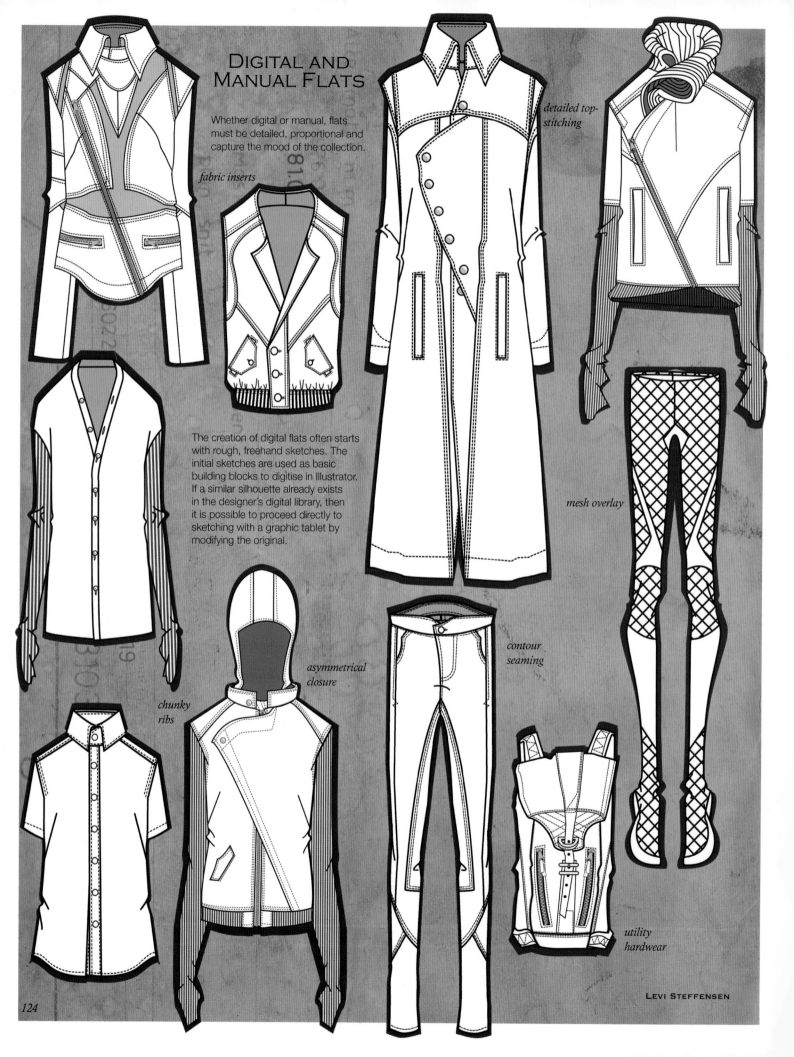

DIGITAL AND MANUAL FLATS

Whether digital or manual, flats must be detailed, proportional and capture the mood of the collection.

fabric inserts

detailed top-stitching

The creation of digital flats often starts with rough, freehand sketches. The initial sketches are used as basic building blocks to digitise in Illustrator. If a similar silhouette already exists in the designer's digital library, then it is possible to proceed directly to sketching with a graphic tablet by modifying the original.

mesh overlay

asymmetrical closure

chunky ribs

contour seaming

utility hardwear

LEVI STEFFENSEN

Wrapped, folded, panelled and blocked, this minimalistic collection is driven by the geometric lines and shapes of paper origami. All about asymmetry, irregular cutouts, oversized velcro closures and sculpted seams, the bold and modern pieces are executed in wool flannel and jersey.

fabric-blocked tops

asymmetrical tabart

modern wrap shift

envelope-waist pants

spiral seam trouser

geometric knits

Flats are manually illustrated in black pen and printed on tinted transparent vellum, then cut out and pasted over a paper collage.

panelled skirt

ANNA KIPER

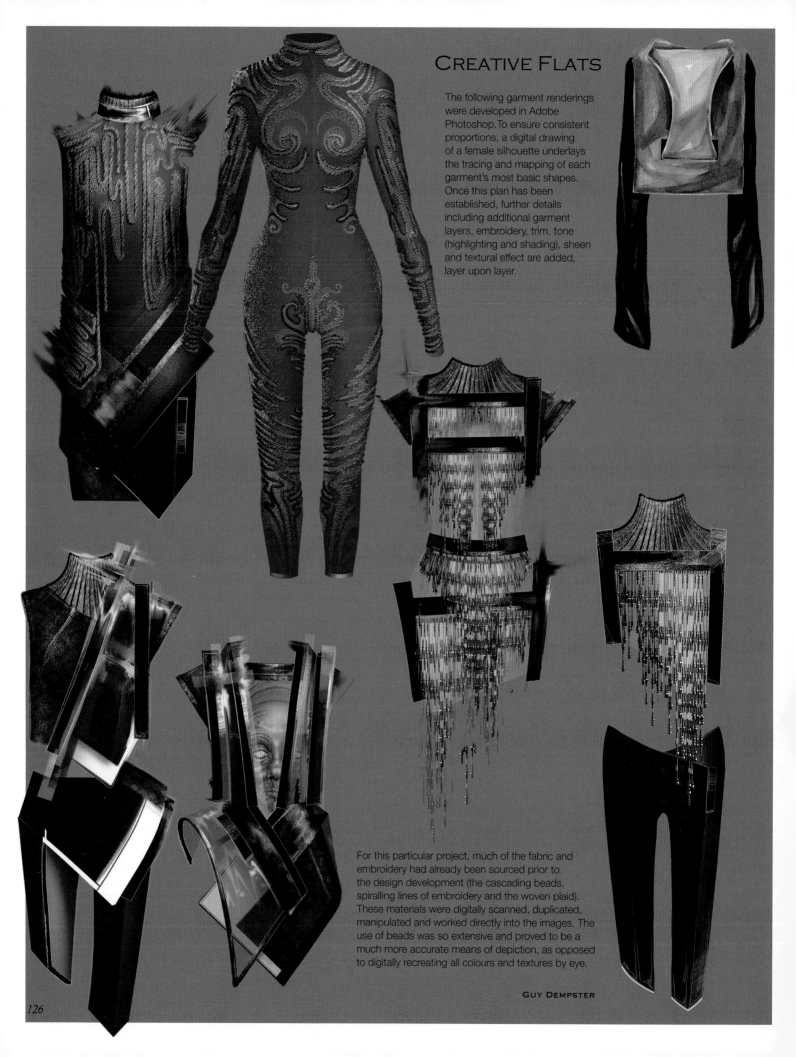

CREATIVE FLATS

The following garment renderings were developed in Adobe Photoshop. To ensure consistent proportions, a digital drawing of a female silhouette underlays the tracing and mapping of each garment's most basic shapes. Once this plan has been established, further details including additional garment layers, embroidery, trim, tone (highlighting and shading), sheen and textural effect are added, layer upon layer.

For this particular project, much of the fabric and embroidery had already been sourced prior to the design development (the cascading beads, spiralling lines of embroidery and the woven plaid). These materials were digitally scanned, duplicated, manipulated and worked directly into the images. The use of beads was so extensive and proved to be a much more accurate means of depiction, as opposed to digitally recreating all colours and textures by eye.

GUY DEMPSTER

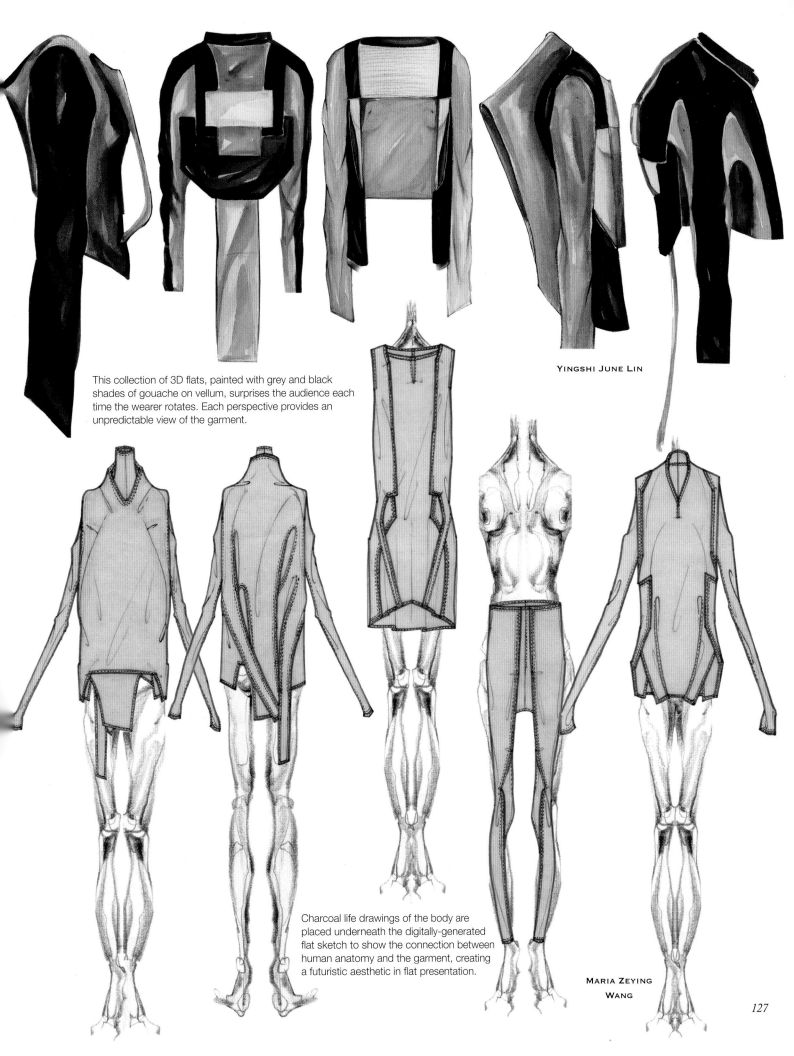

This collection of 3D flats, painted with grey and black shades of gouache on vellum, surprises the audience each time the wearer rotates. Each perspective provides an unpredictable view of the garment.

YINGSHI JUNE LIN

Charcoal life drawings of the body are placed underneath the digitally-generated flat sketch to show the connection between human anatomy and the garment, creating a futuristic aesthetic in flat presentation.

MARIA ZEYING WANG

127

Since flat sketches are rapidly becoming one of the main design development and presentation tools, the traditional style of a clean line, carefully crafted technical sketch is being taken to a new level. Artistic flats often express the mood and design philosophy of the collection, going far beyond a precise representation of the garment.

DESIGN VISION AND FLATS

The deconstructed nature of these jackets is vividly expressed by the collage. Images of the existing garments were taken apart with pieces rearranged in different ways, creating unexpected variations.

SUNGHEE KIM

*grosgrain
and interlining*

Classic tailoring is slightly reconstructed and styled with leather
straps and occasional lingerie pieces. These flats are sketched with
white pencil on black paper or black on grey, and lightly touched
with gouache. The timeless beauty of haberdashery and custom
dressmaking is expressed in elegant details.

ANNA KIPER

DEVELOPING COLLECTIONS

Reflecting the designer's creative vision, the portfolio should contain a few carefully crafted and well-thought-out collections.

While showcasing an original design sensibility and presentation style, collections should be structured using the following steps: inspiration and mood, research and design studies, execution, and then styling and presentation of the final looks.

1. The 'Blue Moment' collection is inspired by the 1920s La Garçonne movement, liberated Jazz Age beauties, seduction and elegance; the atmosphere of a chic and decadently lavish lifestyle: expensive restaurants, sparkling crystals, silver wear and cigarette smoke.

2. The vision of a muse was captured in a photoshoot with a model dressed in exquisite tailoring mixed with lingerie. Timeless beauty is found in an embroidered skull cap and beads on bare skin. Snapshots of the styled model are used for mood, and fabric boards to illustrate the ideal customer.

3. After the mood and general vision of the collection is set, deeper research is conducted, including inspirational images, fabric, trim and colour references.

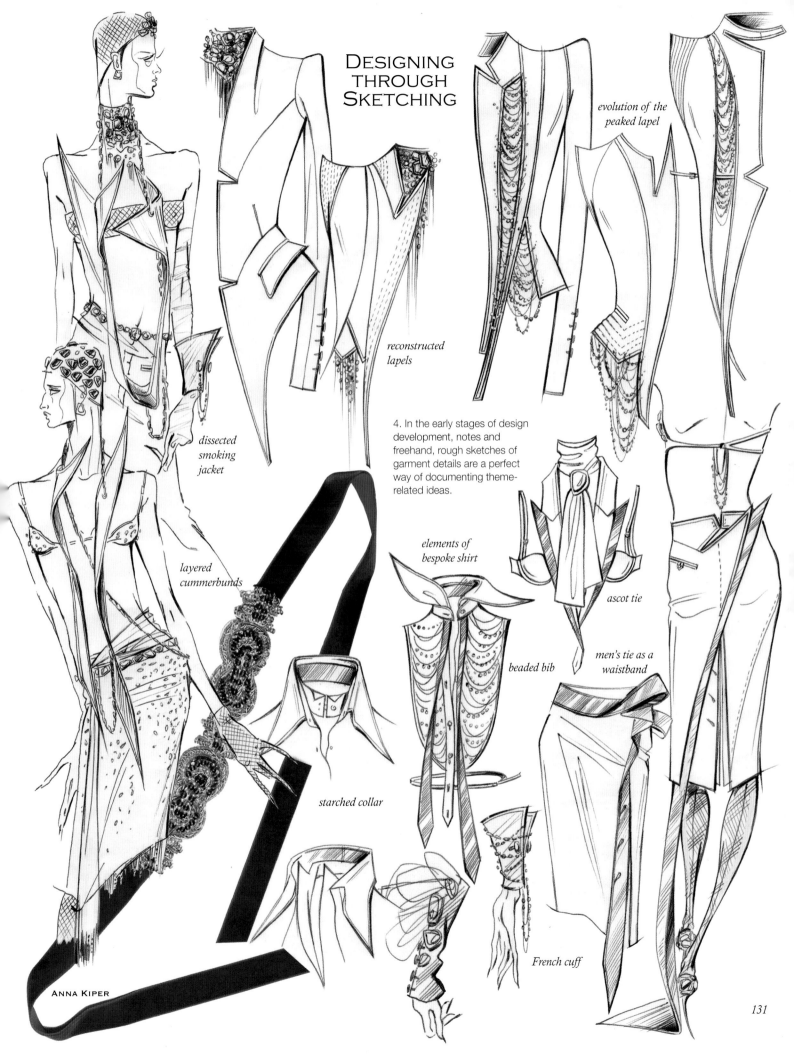

DESIGNING THROUGH SKETCHING

evolution of the peaked lapel

reconstructed lapels

dissected smoking jacket

4. In the early stages of design development, notes and freehand, rough sketches of garment details are a perfect way of documenting theme-related ideas.

elements of bespoke shirt

layered cummerbunds

ascot tie

beaded bib

men's tie as a waistband

starched collar

French cuff

ANNA KIPER

131

5. Notes, comments or lists of key words related to the story help designers to stay focused and turn an abstract inspiration into tangible research and design studies. Illustrating design ideas through quick, small figure sketches, called thumbnails or croquis, is an effective and practical way to document the creative thought process. The thumbnail sketches don't have to be detailed or fully rendered but they should contain just enough information to clearly communicate garment styles, silhouettes and proportions.

- Seductive
- Sensual
- Provocative
- Revealing
- Elegant
- Liberated
- Androgynous

Looks, sketched free hand with black bold pen and lightly touched with blue and grey markers, aside from providing design direction, express the unique attitude and mood of the desirable customer.

Key Fabrics: *Men's suiting pinstripes, velvet, snakeskin, beaded chiffon, mesh, tulle and net.*

Blue is the key colour accent, highlighting grey and black.

Leather straps, tuxedo elements, exposed lingerie, tailored structures and soft drapes, transparency, oversized glass beads and crystals all come together into a dramatic decadent style.

ANNA KIPER

133

twisted
and
tied skirt

multi-strap bra

bias-cut
chiffon blouse

satin-trimmed
top collar

velvet
straps

beaded
leggings

exposed
garter belt

fishnet
stockings

men's tie as
a waistband

flap with trapunto stitch

6. Sewing sample and prototype development, as well as fabric manipulations, allow for the 3D testing of the design theory, bringing the concepts to life. Carefully crafted garment details, executed in an appropriate fabric and placed next to sketches, become a vital part of the design presentation. Focusing in on the smallest nuances, such as decorative stitchings, fabric inserts and hardwear, translates design sketches into the commercial world of garment production.

chiffon-trim sleeve vent

coat on bare skin

deconstructed suits

exposed bra

tulle petticoat

peaked lapel

lingerie merged with tailoring

ANNA KIPER

135

*Design edits
and final looks*

*Watercolour and
gold gouache*

Original snapshots
of a specifically styled
model, or painting and
collaging experiments
with existing images
will help envision a
mood, beauty and a
model's attitude for the
final presentation.

*Brush pen and
copper pitt pen*

7. A few distinct
looks are selected to
be fully rendered for
the final presentation.
Fabrics, including
colour accents, are
finalised for each of
the selected styles.

ANNA KIPER

8. Beauty and accessory
ideas are developed
through sketch studies,
which often include media
testing and exploration.

*Markers, eye shadows
and Le Pen as a final
media choice.*

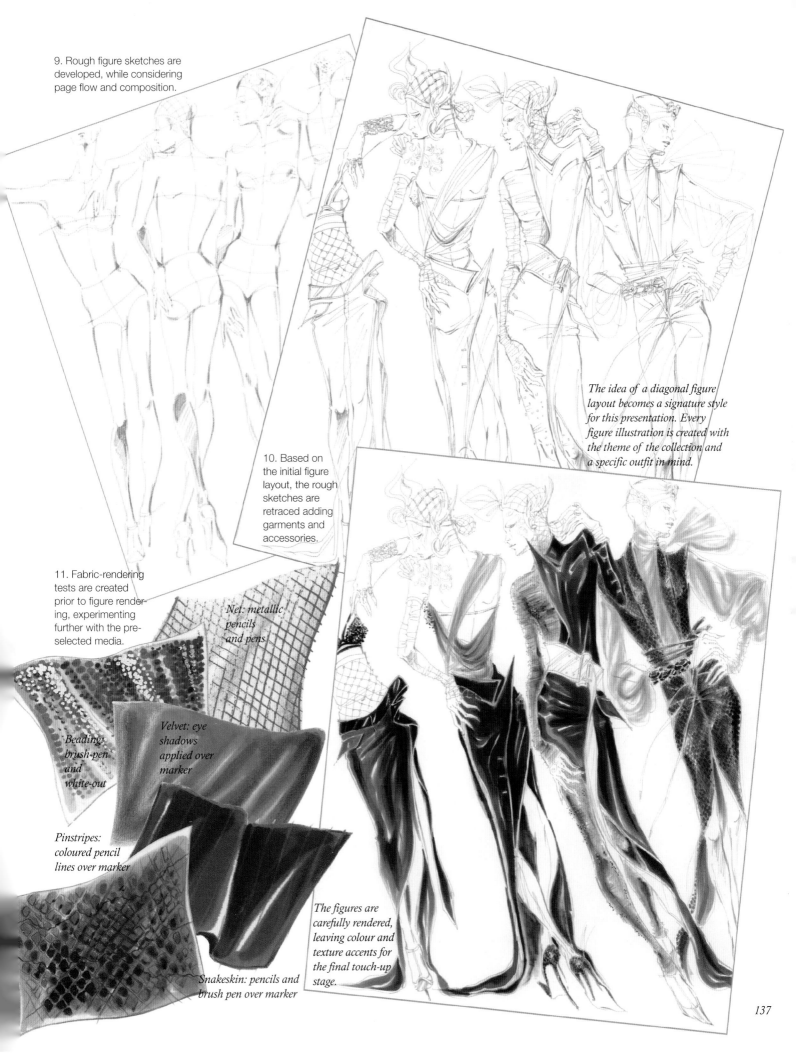

9. Rough figure sketches are developed, while considering page flow and composition.

The idea of a diagonal figure layout becomes a signature style for this presentation. Every figure illustration is created with the theme of the collection and a specific outfit in mind.

10. Based on the initial figure layout, the rough sketches are retraced adding garments and accessories.

11. Fabric-rendering tests are created prior to figure rendering, experimenting further with the pre-selected media.

Net: metallic pencils and pens

Beading: brush-pen and white-out

Velvet: eye shadows applied over marker

Pinstripes: coloured pencil lines over marker

Snakeskin: pencils and brush pen over marker

The figures are carefully rendered, leaving colour and texture accents for the final touch-up stage.

137

12. Illustrated final looks are outlined with lavender Le Pen, rendered with markers, eye shadows and highlighted with metallic and brush pen touch-ups.

Back-view figures are essential for designs with important details in the back of the garment.

Detailed, expressive sketches allow for the presentation, and even sale, of collections before the actual garment samples are created, often saving time and resources.

The seductive mix of sheers, exposed lingerie and deconstructed tailoring, styled with beaded caps, and Charleston ankle-strap pointy heels, creates the mood of modern, nostalgic fantasy.

ANNA KIPER

For some designers sketching is a major part of the design process, and the main way to communicate design ideas. For others the 'language' of the fabric or yarn manipulations is as expressive as a fashion sketch. These designers endlessly study and document various design possibilities in 3D. They drape, mold, manipulate and deconstruct textiles, discovering the best ideas through experimentation and accidents. Snapshots of 3D-design formations in stages often serve as an alternative to the traditional designer sketch.

Twisted yarn samples are an innovative option for design thumbnails.

PAULA CHENG

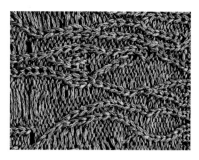

DESIGNING THROUGH TEXTILE MANIPULATION

This nature-inspired collection originates from a deep fascination with the formation of loops, stitches and complex knitting structures. From the growth of tree branches, to the twisting and interweaving patterns of tree barks, the images evoke words such as: formation, invasion, dominance, persistence, movement and infestation.

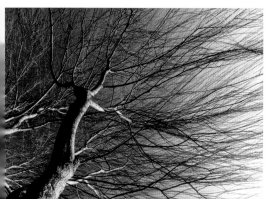

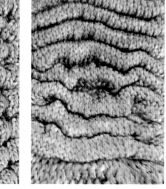

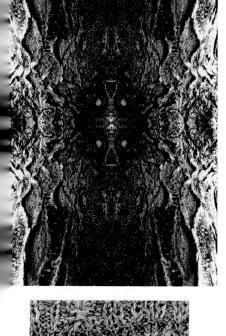

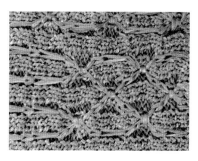

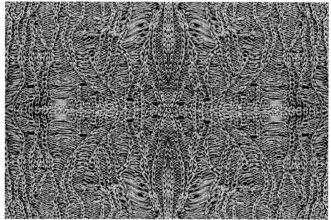

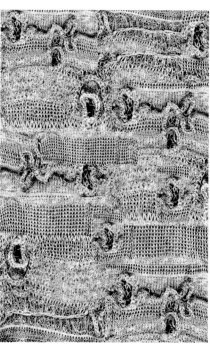

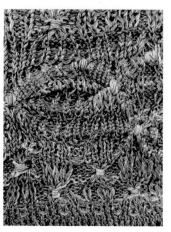

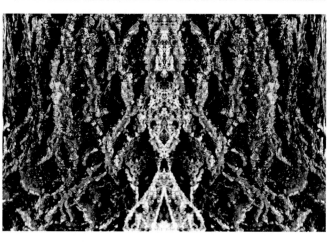

The initial design process evolved through journal studies including photographs of nature, images and words associated with knitting, yarns and textures. Instead of cutting and sewing patterns to apply to the human form, knits can be 'grown' onto the body in a non-uniform way.

Exploration of craft techniques mimic growth in nature. Fibres are manipulated and yarn textures and colours are collaged to create organic shapes and amorphous patterns.

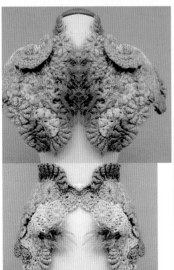

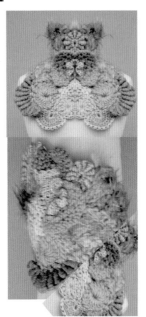

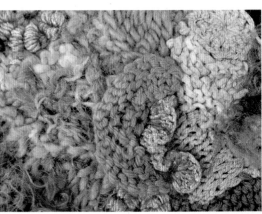

Intertwining fibres and yarns through knitting, crocheting, embroidery, and twisting complex 3D structures.

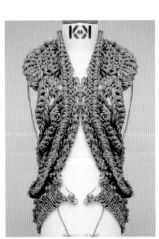

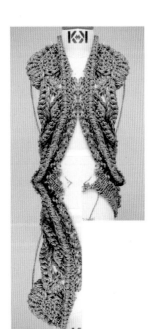

PAULA CHENG

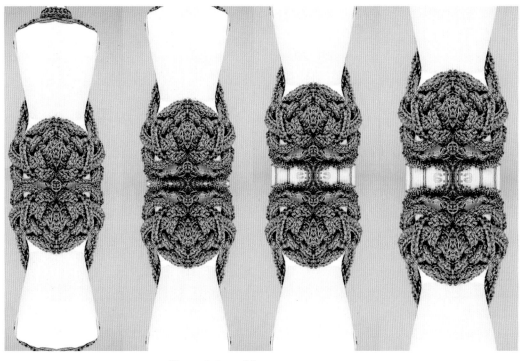

The next stage of the design process was the exploration of various knitting techniques, fibre manipulations and colour story development through hand yarn dying and tinting. Since the patterns derive from the organic shapes and lines of trees and branches, they require more than just the copying of knitting patterns. Instead, it was a long process of cross-referencing to translate the amorphous patterns of nature into knit samples. Additionally elevating the surface of flat fabrics by short-rowing, tucking and manipulating the knits with hand and machine knitting.

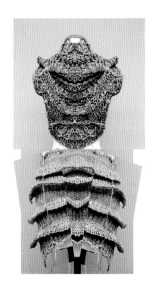

These imaginative and exotic garments evoke the authentic nature of a mature tree trunk, with its complex texture and simple shape. A professional photoshoot of the finished samples with an exotic model complements the concept and mood, and is an effective way to present the final silhouettes. The line-up of the beautifully styled looks in the portfolio will stand out as a modern and professional summary of the creative process.

The use of the 'mirroring' technique creates an unnatural, fantastical symmetry, infusing the garments with a primal element while showcasing the beauty of intricate detailing.

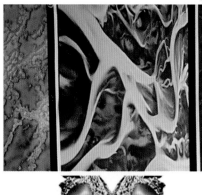

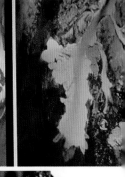

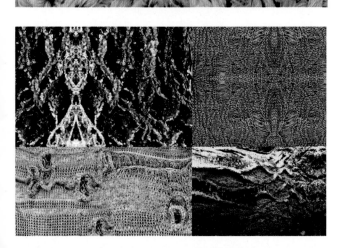

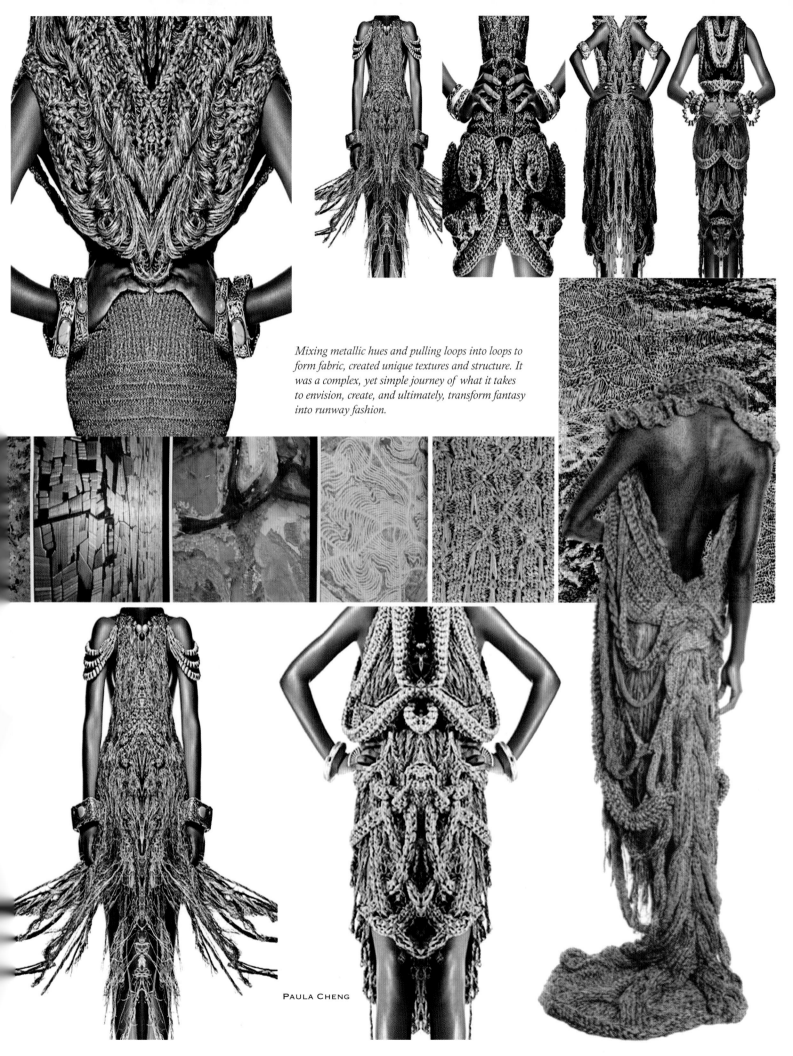

Mixing metallic hues and pulling loops into loops to form fabric, created unique textures and structure. It was a complex, yet simple journey of what it takes to envision, create, and ultimately, transform fantasy into runway fashion.

PAULA CHENG

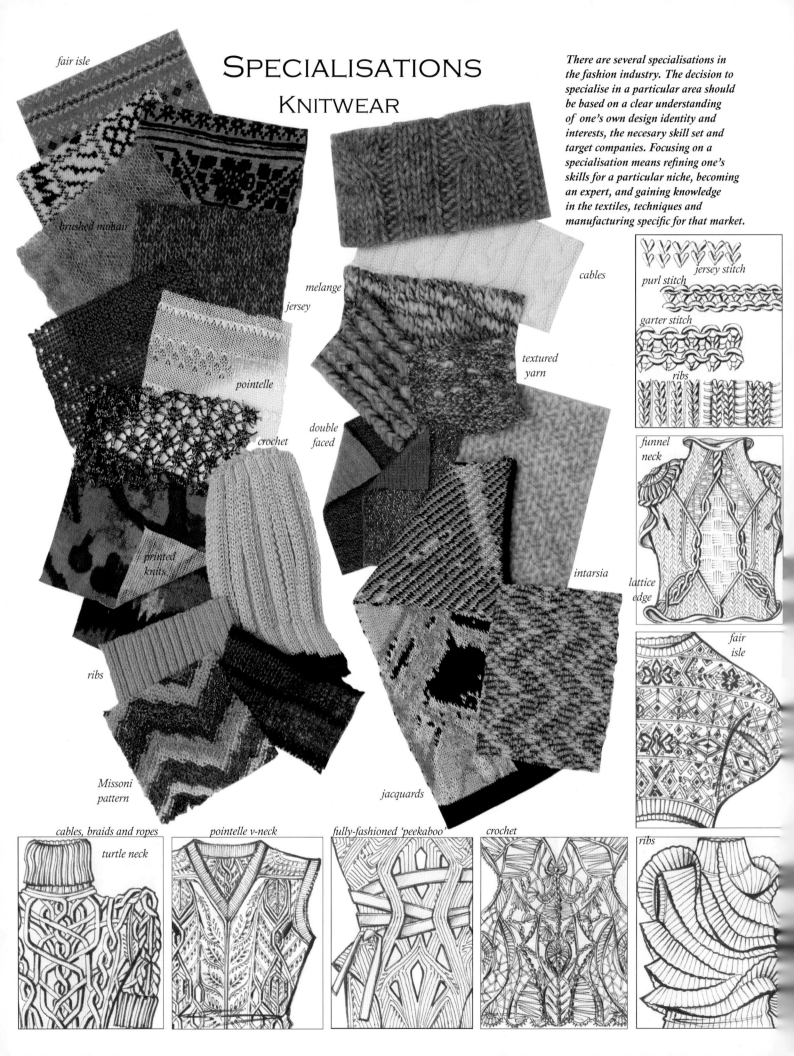

SPECIALISATIONS
KNITWEAR

There are several specialisations in the fashion industry. The decision to specialise in a particular area should be based on a clear understanding of one's own design identity and interests, the necesary skill set and target companies. Focusing on a specialisation means refining one's skills for a particular niche, becoming an expert, and gaining knowledge in the textiles, techniques and manufacturing specific for that market.

fair isle

brushed mohair

melange
jersey

pointelle

crochet

printed knits

ribs

Missoni pattern

cables

textured yarn

double faced

intarsia

jacquards

jersey stitch
purl stitch
garter stitch
ribs

funnel neck

lattice edge

fair isle

cables, braids and ropes
turtle neck

pointelle v-neck

fully-fashioned 'peekaboo'

crochet

ribs

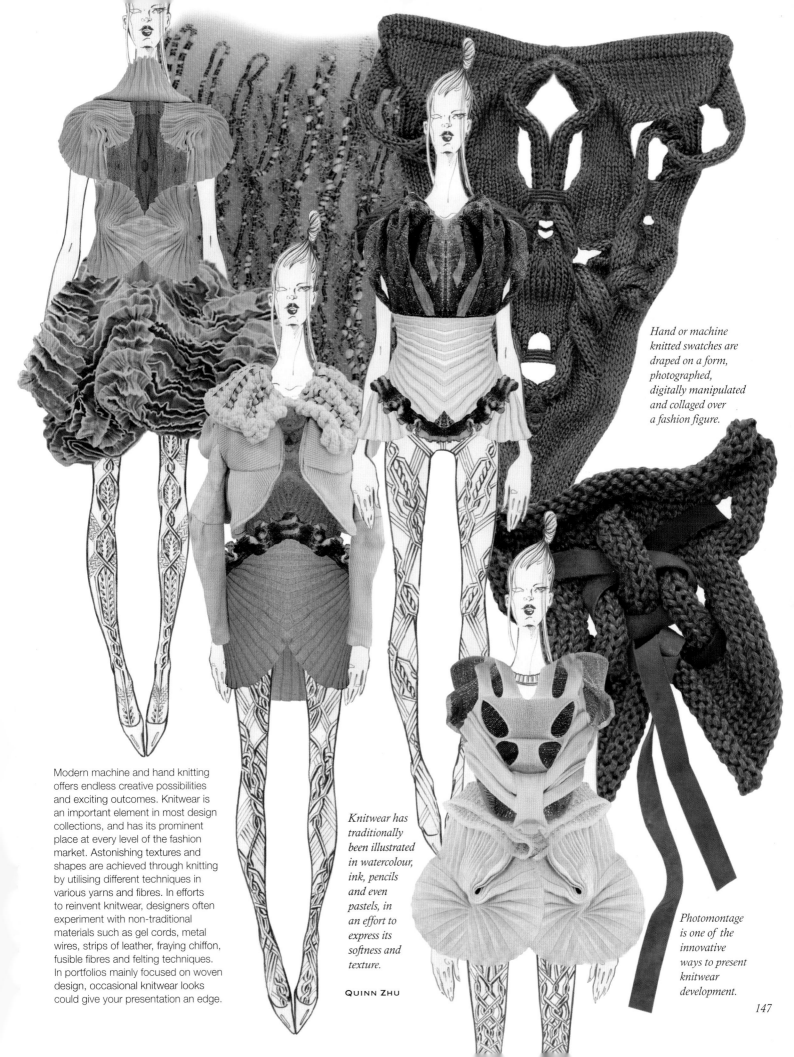

Hand or machine knitted swatches are draped on a form, photographed, digitally manipulated and collaged over a fashion figure.

Modern machine and hand knitting offers endless creative possibilities and exciting outcomes. Knitwear is an important element in most design collections, and has its prominent place at every level of the fashion market. Astonishing textures and shapes are achieved through knitting by utilising different techniques in various yarns and fibres. In efforts to reinvent knitwear, designers often experiment with non-traditional materials such as gel cords, metal wires, strips of leather, fraying chiffon, fusible fibres and felting techniques. In portfolios mainly focused on woven design, occasional knitwear looks could give your presentation an edge.

Knitwear has traditionally been illustrated in watercolour, ink, pencils and even pastels, in an effort to express its softness and texture.

QUINN ZHU

Photomontage is one of the innovative ways to present knitwear development.

147

ARCHITECTURAL KNITS

This collection features pieces inspired by organic shapes and fractal elements. Each garment wraps around the body, creating a sense of infinite movement. Intricate seams, jacquards and pointelles imitate complex architectural details.

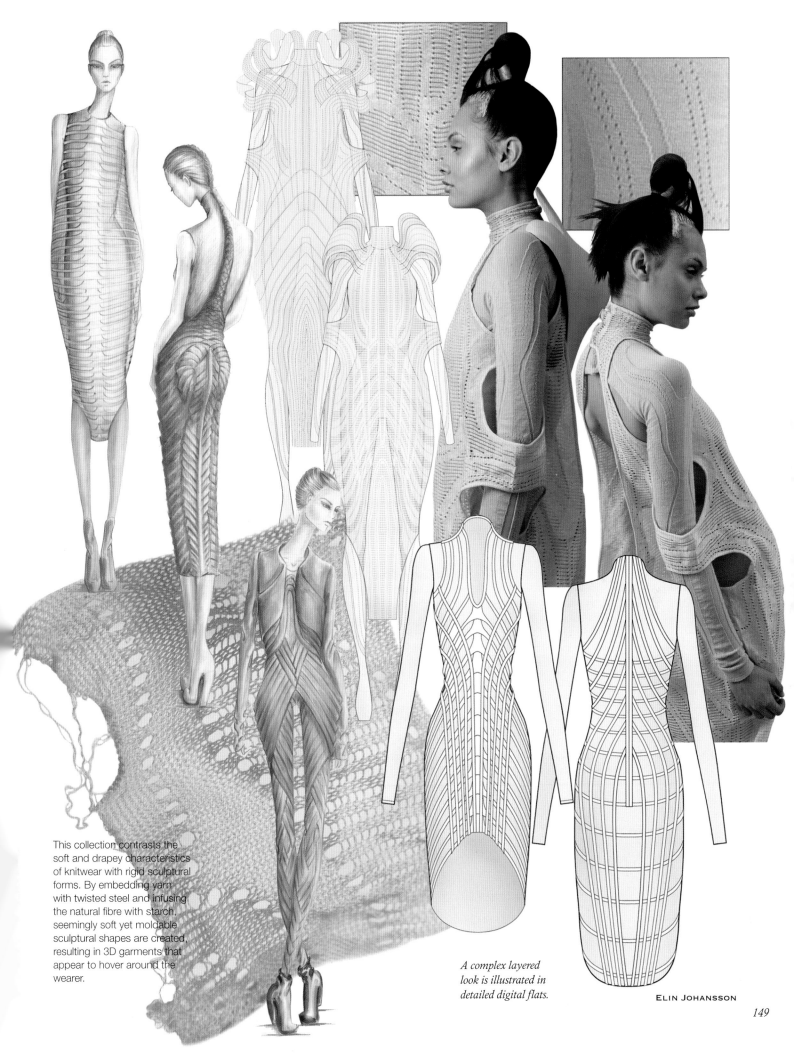

This collection contrasts the soft and drapey characteristics of knitwear with rigid sculptural forms. By embedding yarn with twisted steel and infusing the natural fibre with starch, seemingly soft yet moldable sculptural shapes are created, resulting in 3D garments that appear to hover around the wearer.

A complex layered look is illustrated in detailed digital flats.

ELIN JOHANSSON

149

The styles evolve and morph through different stages using both draping and digital manipulations.

JESSICA VELEZ

Metamorphosis

This collection is knitted using no instructions and no sketches, therefore having no boundaries. Liberally draped hand-knitted swatches are merged into various forms to find the best line and shape on the body. One swatch alone creates an endless array of designs that gradually and organically mutate from one design to another. As a result, any original swatch development presents endless design variations that each hold the same continuous characteristics of form and line. Traditional knitwear is reinterpreted with elements of draping and haute couture sewing techniques. The inspiration from nature and sea life is reflected in intricate surface textures and engineered stitch placement. Ultimately, creative work should evoke emotion and grant creative individualism to the wearer.

DANCING KNITS

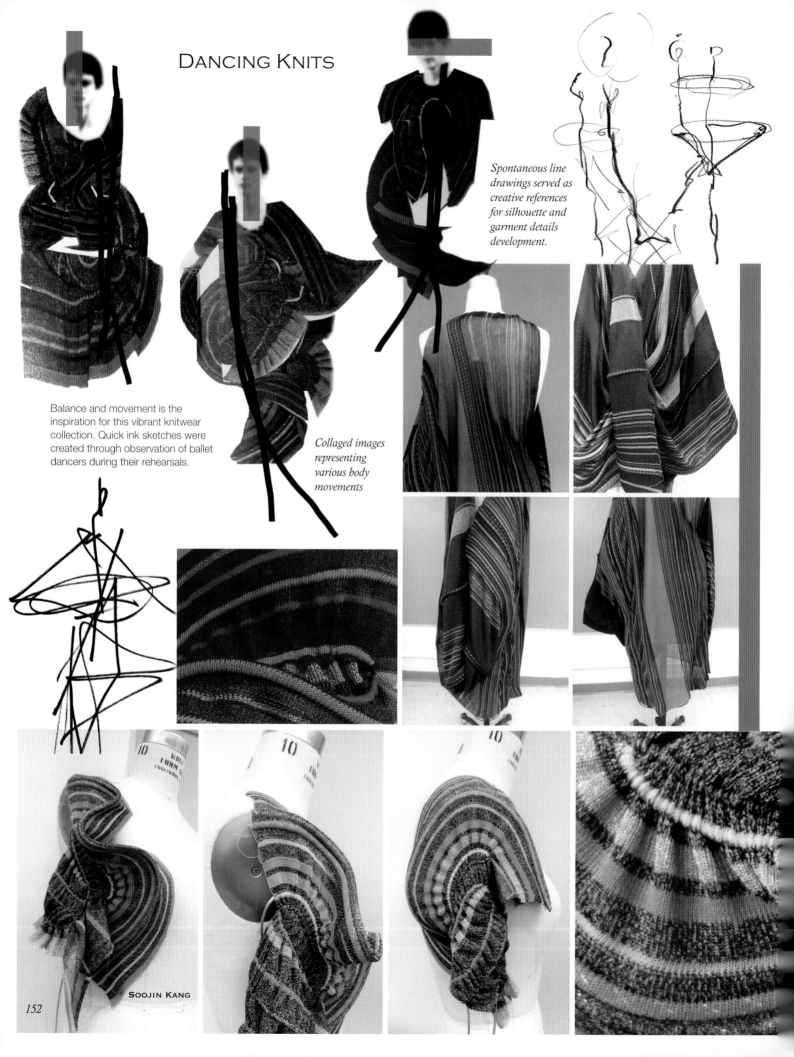

Spontaneous line drawings served as creative references for silhouette and garment details development.

Balance and movement is the inspiration for this vibrant knitwear collection. Quick ink sketches were created through observation of ballet dancers during their rehearsals.

Collaged images representing various body movements

SOOJIN KANG

In the early stages of the knitting process the general garment shape was developed before it was randomly smocked, gathered and twisted. This fun vibrant collection was created using industry knitting machines in combination with some manual techniques, such as tubular and short-row knitting. The cotton and luminex yarns are highly twisted, therefore, they have a bias effect when used in a single knitting bed. Those effects were considered during the design process by carefully placing yarn and the striped portions of the garment. By adjusting those drawstrings, the length and the shape of the garment changes dramatically.

The silhouette of the garments can be adjusted by the built-in drawstrings. The different character of the coloured yarns creates contours in the garment, expressing the movement of dance.

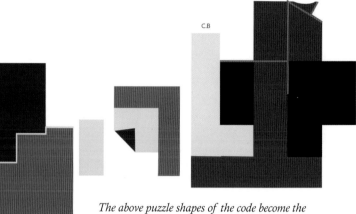

CODE/DECODE KNITWEAR

QR coding was the inspiration for this knitwear collection. The rhythm of the code was translated into colour blocks and large patterns. The idea was transformed into a fine intarsia knitwear collection. Neon accents were used as pipings to highlight the geometric and futuristic mood.

The above puzzle shapes of the code become the actual garment patterns draped in jersey once they are linked together.

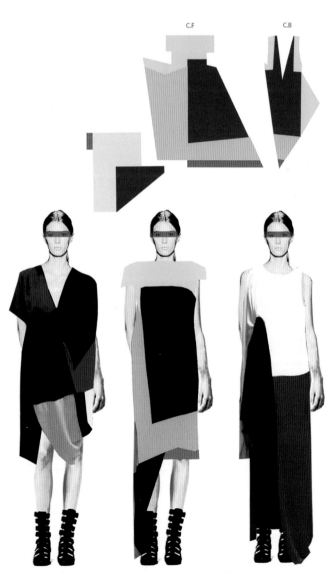

As alternatives to design sketches, figures are photomontaged with draping studies of the garments.

This complex fabric puzzle is the same shape as the one draped on the form to the right.

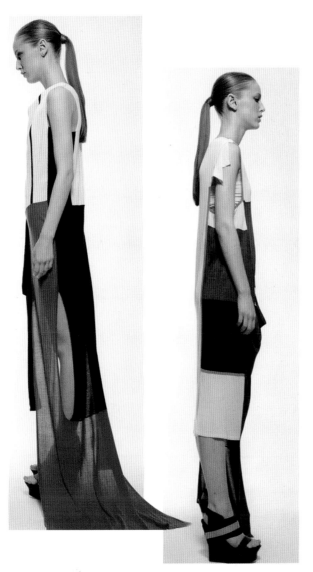

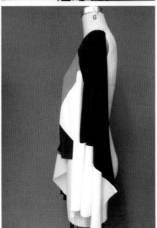

The preliminary step of the design development was the cut-and-sew of jersey fabric presented on the model line-up on the previous page and to the left. All of the final pieces, presented above, have been knitted in a fully-fashioned manner with the intarsia technique executed on a computer knitting machine.

The primary colours, neutralised with black and white, serve as a well-balanced foundation for graphic colour blocking.

Modern art, specifically the works of Piet Mondrian, serve as an influence for the general aesthetic and the edgy mood of the collection.

SOOJIN KANG

ACTIVEWEAR

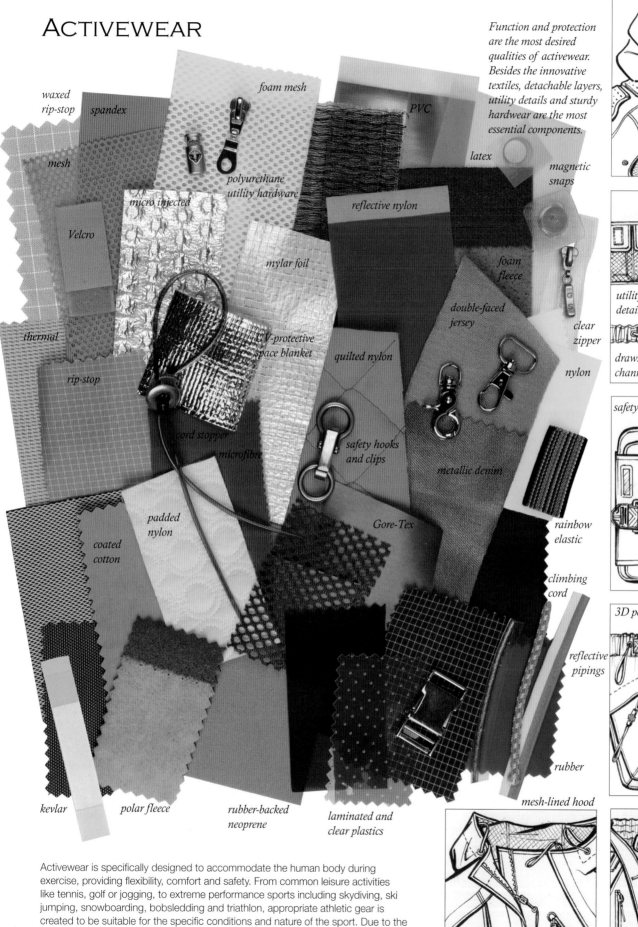

waxed rip-stop

spandex

mesh

Velcro

micro injected

foam mesh

polyurethane utility hardware

mylar foil

thermal

rip-stop

UV-protective space blanket

cord stopper

microfibre

quilted nylon

safety hooks and clips

PVC

latex

magnetic snaps

reflective nylon

foam fleece

double-faced jersey

clear zipper

nylon

metallic denim

rainbow elastic

climbing cord

reflective pipings

rubber

coated cotton

padded nylon

Gore-Tex

kevlar

polar fleece

rubber-backed neoprene

laminated and clear plastics

mesh-lined hood

Function and protection are the most desired qualities of activewear. Besides the innovative textiles, detachable layers, utility details and sturdy hardware are the most essential components.

rolled-in hood

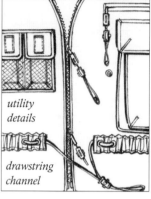

utility details

drawstring channel

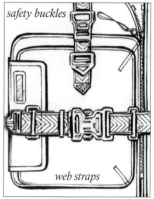

safety buckles

web straps

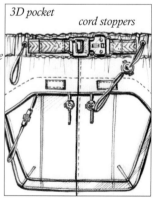

3D pocket

cord stoppers

reflective pipings

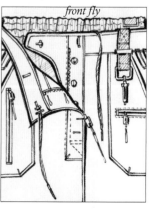

front fly

Activewear is specifically designed to accommodate the human body during exercise, providing flexibility, comfort and safety. From common leisure activities like tennis, golf or jogging, to extreme performance sports including skydiving, ski jumping, snowboarding, bobsledding and triathlon, appropriate athletic gear is created to be suitable for the specific conditions and nature of the sport. Due to the technological advancements of the past decades, a number of high-performance materials have been created from synthetically produced fibres to ensure elasticity and strength, such as acetate, nylon, acrylic, polyester, olefin, spandex and kevlar.

Seam-sealed waterproofed mountain jacket.

UV plastic visor

drawstring channel

detachable storm hood

adjustable hood

built-in plastic pads

Velcro

molded shoulder

key holder

padded elbow

waterproof two-way zippers

built-in pocket system

mesh bottle holder

temperature remote control

ventilation gusset

snaps

zip-out inner layer

phone compartment

snow-proofed cuff

utility pockets

elastic-fitted waistband

Velcro strap

These illustrations reflect the laid back lifestyle of a snowboarder.

buckle waist band

padded knee

snow protective layers

Modern high-tech fabrics are virtually indestructible: water-repellant, flame-retardant, wind-proof, insulated, moisture-absorbent, non-tear, non-slip, waxed, rubberised, laminated, heat-sealed, reflective film-coated and even bacteria resistant like nano-textiles.

Figure illustrations by Renée Smith.

Flats by Anna Kiper

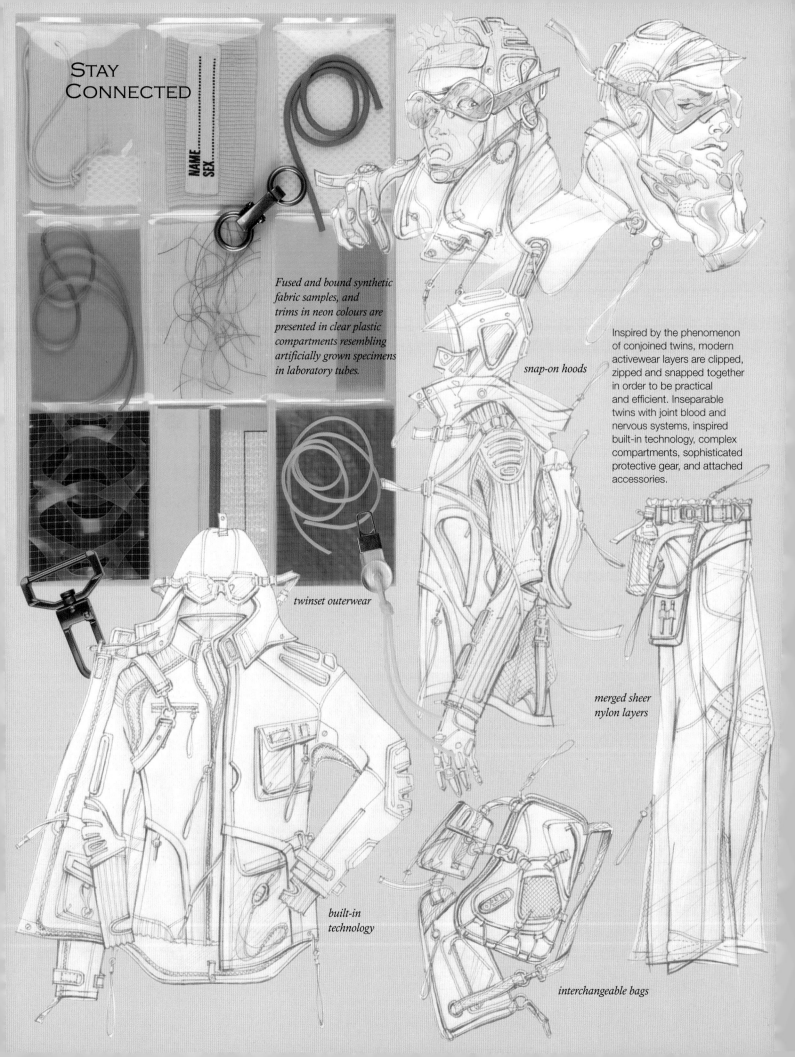

STAY CONNECTED

Fused and bound synthetic fabric samples, and trims in neon colours are presented in clear plastic compartments resembling artificially grown specimens in laboratory tubes.

snap-on hoods

Inspired by the phenomenon of conjoined twins, modern activewear layers are clipped, zipped and snapped together in order to be practical and efficient. Inseparable twins with joint blood and nervous systems, inspired built-in technology, complex compartments, sophisticated protective gear, and attached accessories.

twinset outerwear

merged sheer nylon layers

built-in technology

interchangeable bags

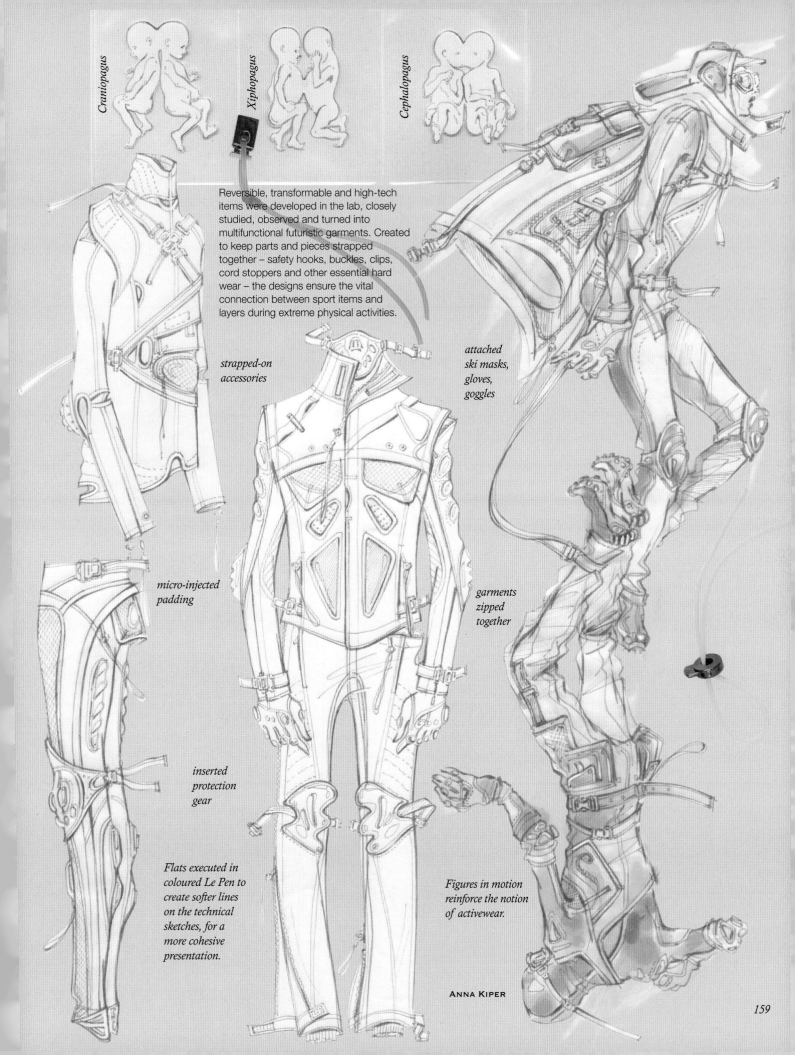

Craniopagus

Xiphopagus

Cephalopagus

Reversible, transformable and high-tech items were developed in the lab, closely studied, observed and turned into multifunctional futuristic garments. Created to keep parts and pieces strapped together – safety hooks, buckles, clips, cord stoppers and other essential hard wear – the designs ensure the vital connection between sport items and layers during extreme physical activities.

strapped-on accessories

attached ski masks, gloves, goggles

micro-injected padding

garments zipped together

inserted protection gear

Flats executed in coloured Le Pen to create softer lines on the technical sketches, for a more cohesive presentation.

Figures in motion reinforce the notion of activewear.

ANNA KIPER

159

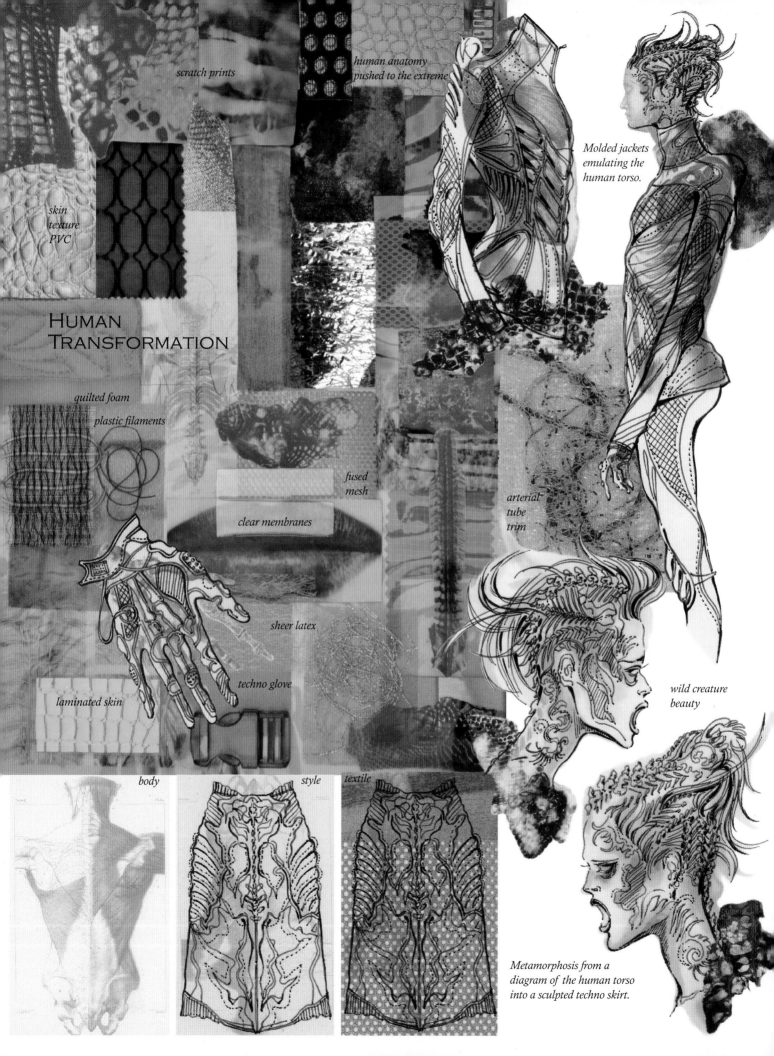

scratch prints

human anatomy
pushed to the extreme

Molded jackets
emulating the
human torso.

skin
texture
PVC

HUMAN
TRANSFORMATION

quilted foam

plastic filaments

fused
mesh

clear membranes

arterial
tube
trim

sheer latex

techno glove

laminated skin

wild creature
beauty

body

style

textile

Metamorphosis from a
diagram of the human torso
into a sculpted techno skirt.

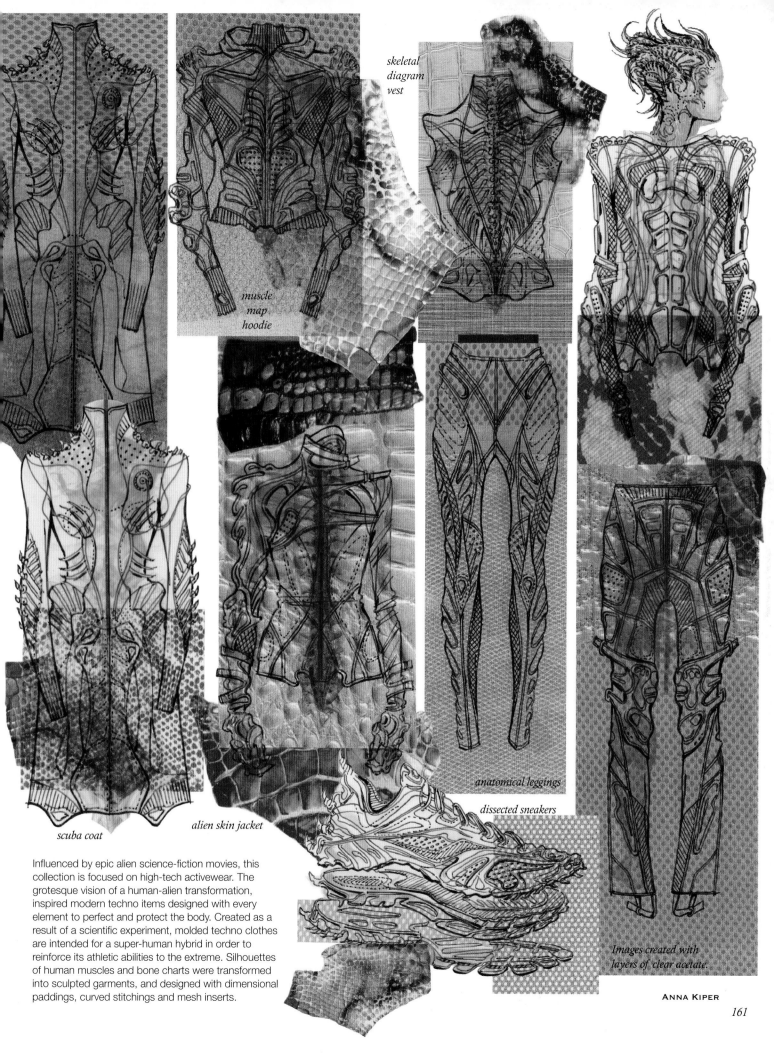

skeletal diagram vest

muscle map hoodie

anatomical leggings

dissected sneakers

scuba coat

alien skin jacket

Influenced by epic alien science-fiction movies, this collection is focused on high-tech activewear. The grotesque vision of a human-alien transformation, inspired modern techno items designed with every element to perfect and protect the body. Created as a result of a scientific experiment, molded techno clothes are intended for a super-human hybrid in order to reinforce its athletic abilities to the extreme. Silhouettes of human muscles and bone charts were transformed into sculpted garments, and designed with dimensional paddings, curved stitchings and mesh inserts.

Images created with layers of clear acetate.

ANNA KIPER

161

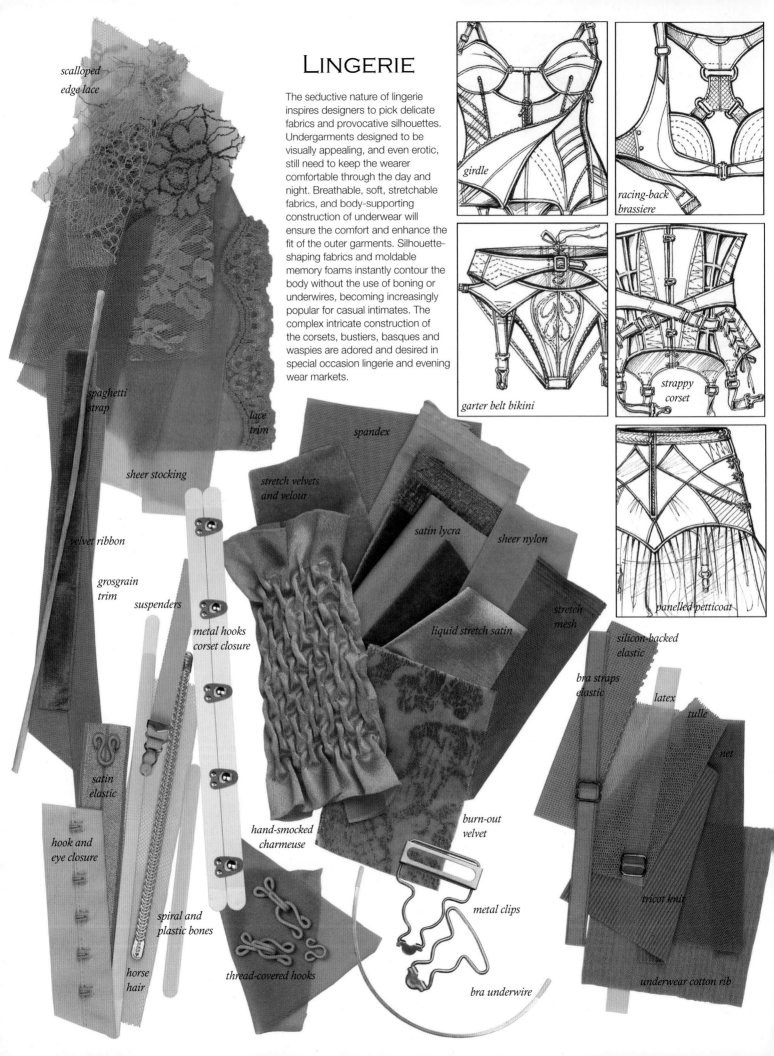

LINGERIE

The seductive nature of lingerie inspires designers to pick delicate fabrics and provocative silhouettes. Undergarments designed to be visually appealing, and even erotic, still need to keep the wearer comfortable through the day and night. Breathable, soft, stretchable fabrics, and body-supporting construction of underwear will ensure the comfort and enhance the fit of the outer garments. Silhouette-shaping fabrics and moldable memory foams instantly contour the body without the use of boning or underwires, becoming increasingly popular for casual intimates. The complex intricate construction of the corsets, bustiers, basques and waspies are adored and desired in special occasion lingerie and evening wear markets.

scalloped edge lace

spaghetti strap

lace trim

sheer stocking

velvet ribbon

grosgrain trim

suspenders

metal hooks corset closure

satin elastic

hook and eye closure

horse hair

spiral and plastic bones

thread-covered hooks

hand-smocked charmeuse

bra underwire

metal clips

burn-out velvet

spandex

stretch velvets and velour

satin lycra

sheer nylon

liquid stretch satin

stretch mesh

silicon-backed elastic

bra straps elastic

latex

tulle

net

tricot knit

underwear cotton rib

girdle

racing-back brassiere

garter belt bikini

strappy corset

panelled petticoat

Despite the restricting fabric choices and limited silhouette options, the lingerie market keeps on surprising customers with the vast array of creative possibilities and innovative design solutions.

The Top Lingerie Fashion Houses:
La Perla, Natori, Agent Provocateur, Victoria's Secret, Bella Bella, Eres, Bordelle, Vagin Pouvoir, Damaris, Allure de Star, Chantelle, Lise Charmel, Spoylt, Aubade, Vagin Pouvoir, Hanky Panky.

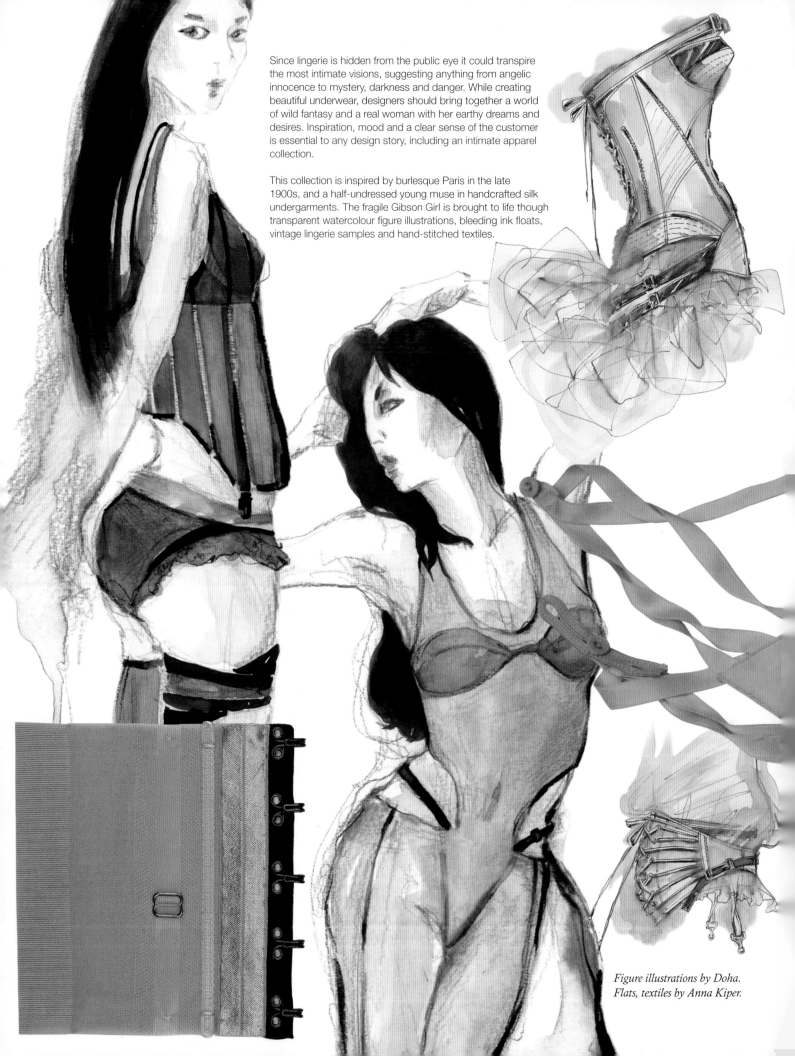

Since lingerie is hidden from the public eye it could transpire the most intimate visions, suggesting anything from angelic innocence to mystery, darkness and danger. While creating beautiful underwear, designers should bring together a world of wild fantasy and a real woman with her earthy dreams and desires. Inspiration, mood and a clear sense of the customer is essential to any design story, including an intimate apparel collection.

This collection is inspired by burlesque Paris in the late 1900s, and a half-undressed young muse in handcrafted silk undergarments. The fragile Gibson Girl is brought to life though transparent watercolour figure illustrations, bleeding ink floats, vintage lingerie samples and hand-stitched textiles.

Figure illustrations by Doha.
Flats, textiles by Anna Kiper.

Bandages, straps,
grosgrain stays,
constricting fan
lacing mixed with
delicate chiffons and
tulle, portray a sense
of innocence that is
about to be shattered
by the harsh realities
of life.

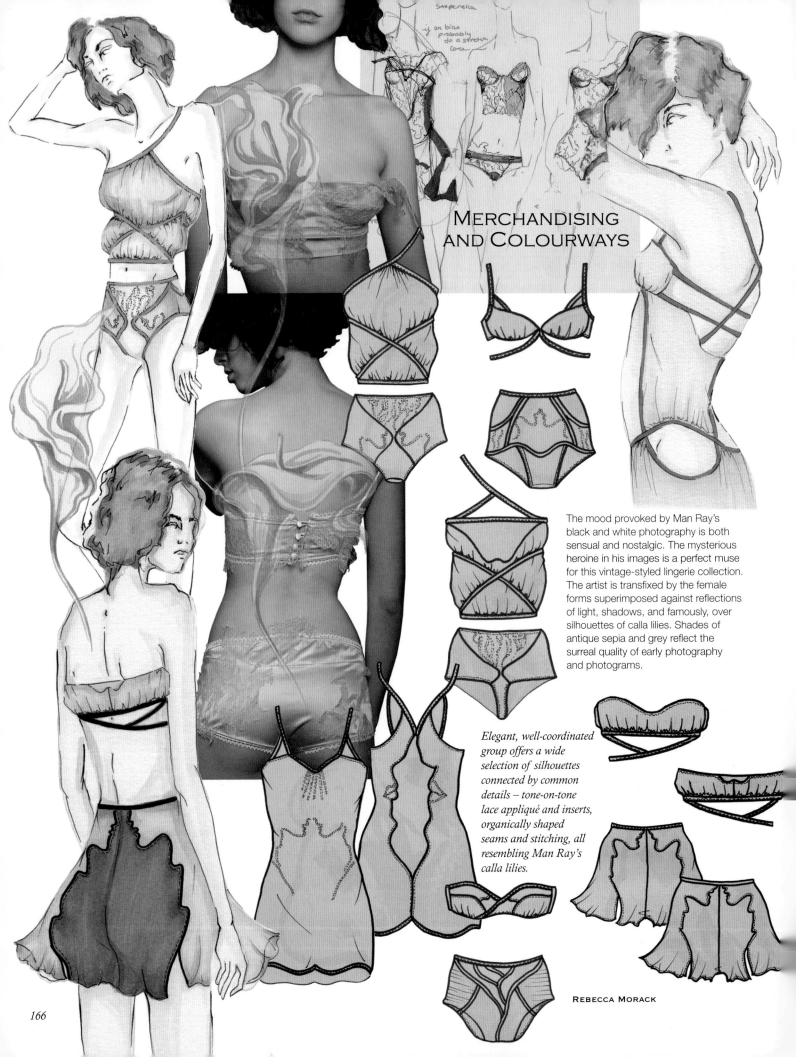

MERCHANDISING AND COLOURWAYS

The mood provoked by Man Ray's black and white photography is both sensual and nostalgic. The mysterious heroine in his images is a perfect muse for this vintage-styled lingerie collection. The artist is transfixed by the female forms superimposed against reflections of light, shadows, and famously, over silhouettes of calla lilies. Shades of antique sepia and grey reflect the surreal quality of early photography and photograms.

Elegant, well-coordinated group offers a wide selection of silhouettes connected by common details – tone-on-tone lace appliqué and inserts, organically shaped seams and stitching, all resembling Man Ray's calla lilies.

REBECCA MORACK

166

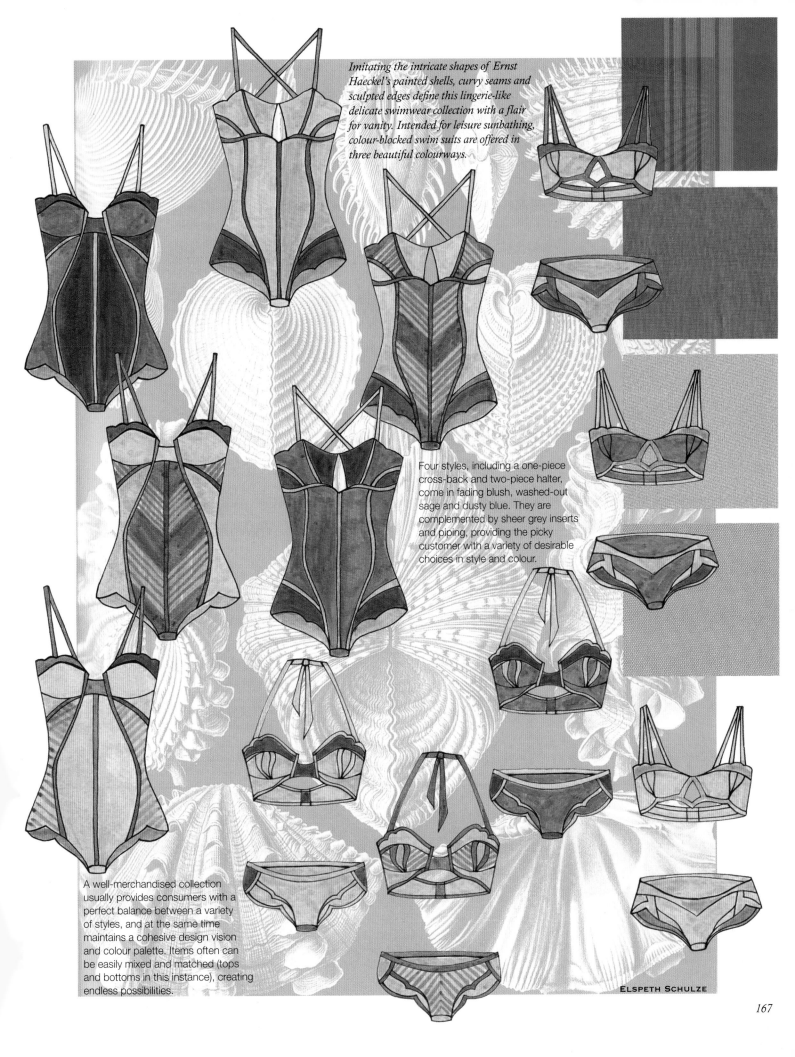

Imitating the intricate shapes of Ernst Haeckel's painted shells, curvy seams and sculpted edges define this lingerie-like delicate swimwear collection with a flair for vanity. Intended for leisure sunbathing, colour-blocked swim suits are offered in three beautiful colourways.

Four styles, including a one-piece cross-back and two-piece halter, come in fading blush, washed-out sage and dusty blue. They are complemented by sheer grey inserts and piping, providing the picky customer with a variety of desirable choices in style and colour.

A well-merchandised collection usually provides consumers with a perfect balance between a variety of styles, and at the same time maintains a cohesive design vision and colour palette. Items often can be easily mixed and matched (tops and bottoms in this instance), creating endless possibilities.

ELSPETH SCHULZE

LINGERIE CATEGORIES

From artisanal to commercial, lingerie is divided into three categories. **Sleepwear** *with robes, pyjamas, after-bath terries, and loungewear.* **Daywear** *consists of basic underwear: panties, bras, camisoles and body shapers. Corsets, basques, petticoats and other mostly structural items commonly worn under bridal and special occasion dresses are called* **Foundations**.

A balanced collection should be well merchandised and include not only a large selection of various items, but offer choices from all lingerie categories.

pyjama top
pull-on pants

camisole

boxer shorts

negligee set

bodysuit shaper

panty shaper

leg smoother

robes and peignoirs

corset

chemise

bustier

tank top

underwire bra

waist cincher

corselet

merry widow

panties briefs

girdle

bikini

teddy

garter belt

petticoats and crinolines

ANNA KIPER

Digital flats executed in Illustrator (opposite page) shows manual floats.

babydoll

contour seam merry widow

push-up bra

The style lines and seams of this medieval architecture inspired collection resemble the arches and domes of Gothic cathedrals. Intricate lace inserts and scalloped edges, as well as the dramatic black and red colour story, represent the faded glory of the forgotten and deteriorated structures.

sheer bodysuit

A RAM SIM

bikini with cover-up

thong

hourglass corset

169

charmeuse

chiffon

seed beads
on printed
chiffon

georgette

organza

ombre and
devore velvets

plush

fluted
pleats

Swarovski
stones

crystal
pleats

embossed
leather

brocade and
jacquard

burn-out
velvet

crushed velvet
and velour

duchess satin

faceted and
bugle beads

taffeta

painted velvet

metallic mesh

dupioni

rhinestones

moiré

silk gauze

paillettes

metallic
sequins

point
d'esprit

lace

metallic
glitter

tulle

From the glamour of red carpet gowns, to special occasion chic layers and cocktail dresses, evening wear is one of the markets that allows for the most creativity and innovation, supported by larger budgets for exclusive fabrics and embellishments. In the haute couture world, fantasy and beauty often come before practicality and comfort, due to its unique and rare usage.

EVENING WEAR

Velvets, brocades and satins embellished with beads and rhinestones create an exclusive, rich fabric story. Ornate jewellery and accessories add a royal touch to the modern, yet elegant clothes.

A magical story is told through watercolour sketches, luxury fabrics, accessories, jewellery and beauty, creating a strong vision of a specific consumer, an event's setting and mood. Victorian era ornamentation and high-status jewels create a romantic narrative.

CARTERIS BROWN

PLEATS AND CUTOUTS

The concept behind this evening wear collection is based on the shape and textures of various plants. The experimental design process included flora research, identifying specific qualities of plants such as symmetry in intricately layered petals, thorns and fine vein structures on leaves. This collection is created from laser-cut pony hair, hand-fringed organza, pleated tulle and leather to emulate the natural qualities and intricate shapes of flowers.

Creating a step-by-step laser-cut leather sculpture.

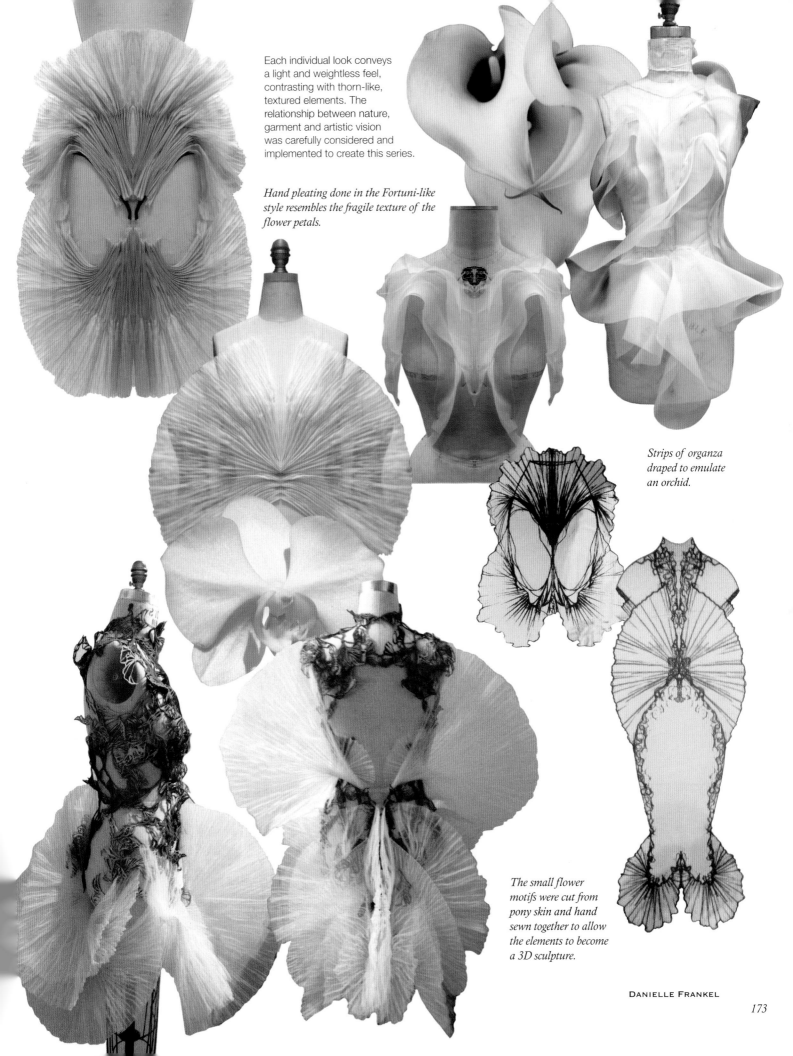

Each individual look conveys a light and weightless feel, contrasting with thorn-like, textured elements. The relationship between nature, garment and artistic vision was carefully considered and implemented to create this series.

Hand pleating done in the Fortuni-like style resembles the fragile texture of the flower petals.

Strips of organza draped to emulate an orchid.

The small flower motifs were cut from pony skin and hand sewn together to allow the elements to become a 3D sculpture.

DANIELLE FRANKEL

173

Two-dimensional line drawings are redefined through the use of wire, and mimicking the technique of artificial flower making. A linear flower drawing and a 3D-wire art piece was molded onto a mannequin as one of the design exercises. Flexible metal wire, chiffon, tulle and soft muslin are creatively manipulated to resemble intricate flower motifs, creating airy sculptures. The step-by-step creative process is documented by a series of snapshots taken during various design stages.

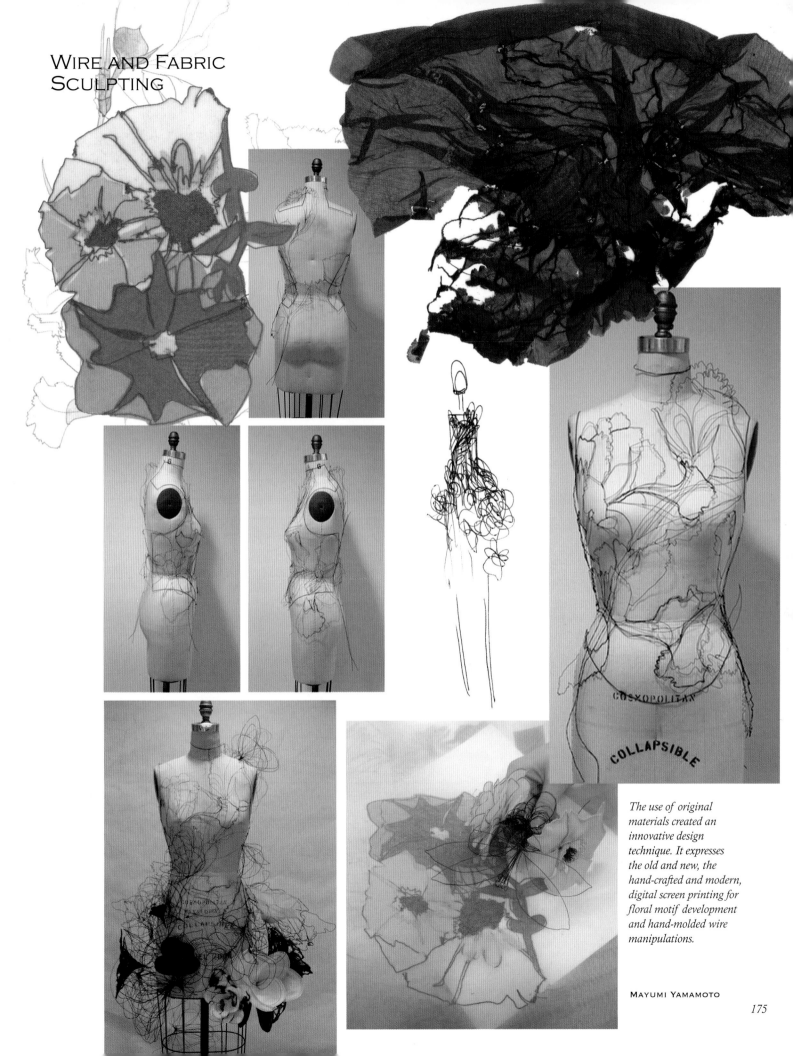

WIRE AND FABRIC
SCULPTING

The use of original materials created an innovative design technique. It expresses the old and new, the hand-crafted and modern, digital screen printing for floral motif development and hand-molded wire manipulations.

MAYUMI YAMAMOTO

175

A dream-ike, feminine image was created by laying different pieces of chiffon with hand-sketched petals on top of a photograph.

Romantic sculptures were created by layering, cascading, smocking and gathering strips of chiffon and georgette cut on the bias. Intricate stitching techniques, wire threading, laser cutting and burned edges were used to create unique details.

The experiment with burning fabric edges was taken a step further by using fire-retardant fabric spray and thread.

LASER CUTS AND BURNED EDGES

The original drapery transitions into the final work through burning and laser-cutting methods. The concepts of fire protection and the destruction of form created an artificial, yet natural beauty. Laser cutting, stitchery and edge-fraying were introduced to the design process to create a new, modern lacing technique.

Illustrations by Anna Kiper.

MAYUMI YAMAMOTO

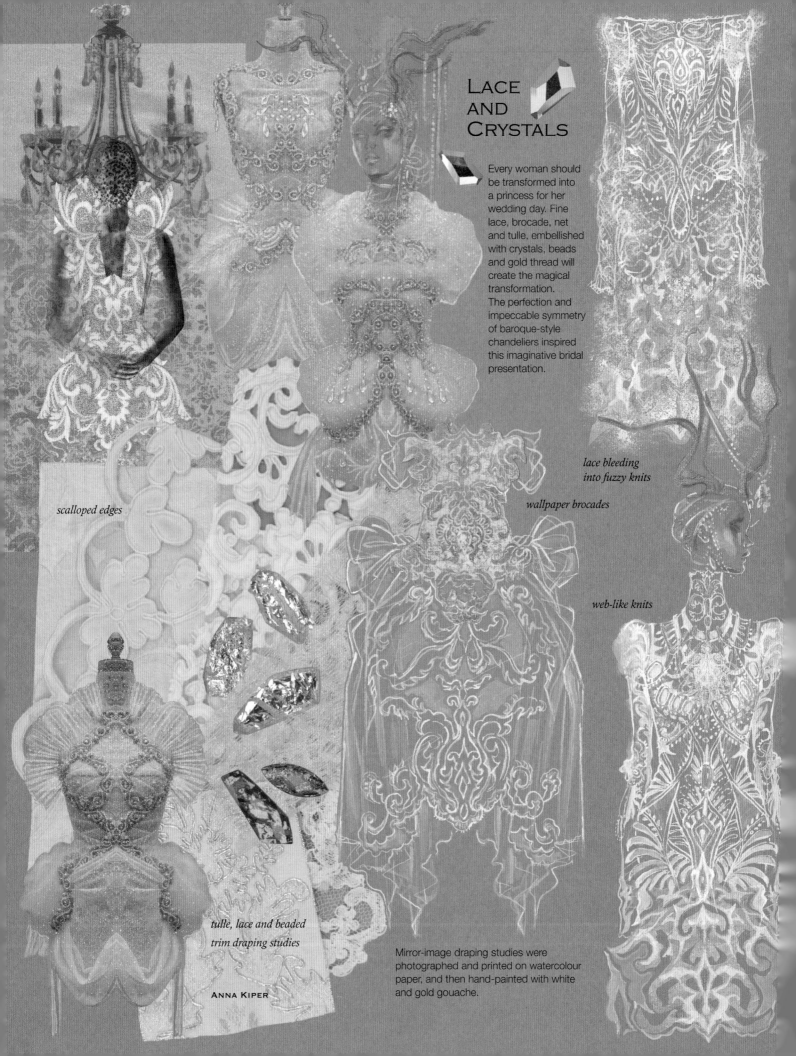

LACE AND CRYSTALS

Every woman should be transformed into a princess for her wedding day. Fine lace, brocade, net and tulle, embellished with crystals, beads and gold thread will create the magical transformation. The perfection and impeccable symmetry of baroque-style chandeliers inspired this imaginative bridal presentation.

lace bleeding into fuzzy knits

scalloped edges

wallpaper brocades

web-like knits

tulle, lace and beaded trim draping studies

ANNA KIPER

Mirror-image draping studies were photographed and printed on watercolour paper, and then hand-painted with white and gold gouache.

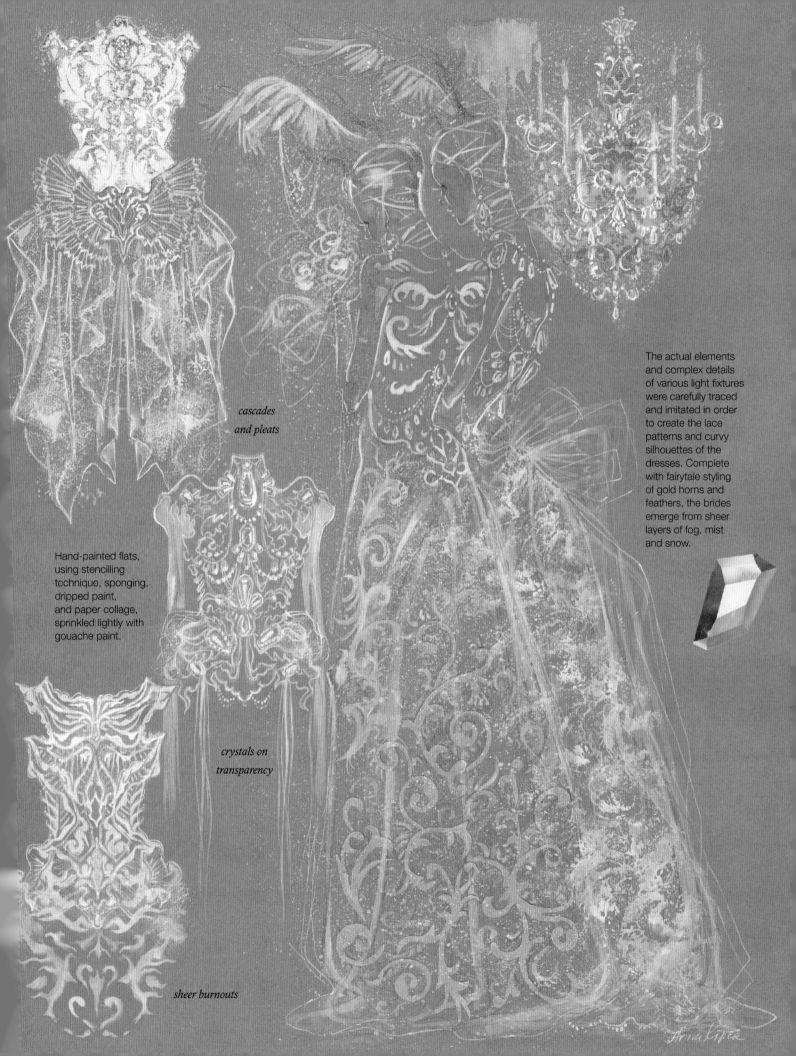

cascades
and pleats

The actual elements and complex details of various light fixtures were carefully traced and imitated in order to create the lace patterns and curvy silhouettes of the dresses. Complete with fairytale styling of gold horns and feathers, the brides emerge from sheer layers of fog, mist and snow.

Hand-painted flats, using stencilling technique, sponging, dripped paint, and paper collage, sprinkled lightly with gouache paint.

crystals on
transparency

sheer burnouts

MENSWEAR

Menswear trends have traditionally evolved at a slower pace, with more conservative textiles, colours and silhouettes. It was only at the turn of last century when the frock coat was replaced with the practical three-piece suit, and the mobile and active lifestyle of the 1920s allowed for the emergence of casual dress. Retro looks of the 40s and 50s, including Teddy Boy skinny jeans, sweater vests, preppy khakis and bright polos, as well as Oxford shirts and navy blazers of the Ivy League style are still very popular today.

The Mod shrunken suit of the 60s influenced the modern metrosexual look. At the same time, Rave, Grunge and Hip-hop cultures of the 80s and 90s paved the way for the baggy jeans, Nike Air Jordans and nylon tracksuits of the contemporary rap style. Recently the dark aesthetic of Rick Owens and Riccardo Tisci emerged, introducing asymmetrical knits and leather layers in subdued colour schemes.

d.cipher fm

Images from trend forecast, d.cipher fm

Menswear Categories:
Black tie / Formal wear
Tailored / Business wear
Sportswear and Separates
Activewear
Outerwear
Loungewear
Underwear

Markets:
Bespoke tailoring
Designer
High-end sportswear
Young contemporary
Casual and street

**Popular
Brands:**
Hugo Boss
Zegna
Dsquared2
Gucci men
A/X Men
Paul Smith
Brioni
Raf Simons
Burberry
Tom Ford
Diesel Men
John Lewis

As modern men focused more on their appearance, the fashion
industry started to expand the various menswear categories.
Many brands opened new menswear lines taking advantage
of the young male demographic by appealing to customers
with creative possibilities and technological innovations in
construction and textiles. Rapidly changing under the influences
of street trends and pop culture, menswear is moving beyond the
traditionally accepted standards of the male image.

ANNA KIPER

Ink outline and marker

NEHA BHATIA

MEN'S ILLUSTRATION STYLES

Stylised, edgy menswear sketches express the young, modern and the eccentric urban man. The concept of traditional, classic menswear has been taken over by a more eclectic and individualistic style.

Designers, including menswear designers, use a variety of visual research materials to carefully develop a signature illustration style portraying their design aesthetic. At the same time the choice of media, figure proportions, and illustration style should reflect a particular customer and vary from collection to collection. In the industry, contemporary menswear illustrations are often created digitally, but paper collage, photomontage, marker and gouache renderings are still very effective and popular techniques.

Gouache and coloured pencils

DIANA CHENG

Pen outline, marker and digital enhancement

DYLAN PAUL
MORAN TAVERNER

Pro-white paint, pencil and photomontage

YOONHEE JOE

Dry brush and gouache

JIHYE MIN

Watercolour and paper collage

JIN HWA LEE

LUXURY SURF

The Spring / Summer Menswear Collection represents a nonchalant, edgy and contemporary style. The collection is inspired by the scenery of rough, black sandstone, the soft, serene ocean, and the clean, tinted blue sky.

PRINT-ON- DENI

The fabrics combine contrasting elements with various textures: lightweight, raw-linen, fine cotton jersey, sandwashed denim and matte-finished crocodile leather with raw edges that emulate the surf. The colours present a contrast between subdued neutrals and bright neons.

Collar as Hoop silhouette

texture

printed denim leggings

plexiglass briefcase

colour-blocked t-shirts

Screen-printed denim, hand-painted canvas, and loosely woven knits inspired by sand, pebbles, and stones. The illustrations were executed in linear ink silhouettes on clear acetate, and superimposed over scraps of textured knits, screen-printed twills and hand-painted leather.

tone-on-tone leather appliqué

SCARLET JANG

*galactic
diagram
stitching*

*spiral seam
easy jeans*

*velcro-strap
moon boots*

These clothes are soft and easy, inspired
by the vast space of the universe. The
fabrics are midnight-blue skies sprinkled
with stardust, top-stitched in white,
resembling constellation diagrams.

*The loose watercolour
sketches convey the feeling
of being suspended in space
and floating along while
escaping gravity.*

ADRIENNE PERLSTEIN

186

CELESTIAL COMFORT

The collection is an exploration into cosmology and the movement of the stars.

multi-layered henley

pull-over blanket pants

space-axis panelled shirt

Seams and garment details are slightly tilted to follow the planetary axes. Pants are dip-dyed to mimic the horizon line of the rising sun. Easy layering provides protection and comfort.

187

OUTDOOR LAYERS

A late fall trip to Portland, Maine formed the basis of inspiration for this men's casual outerwear collection. The unique freehand sketches are flawed, some abstracted, some focused. This is a visual journal, an artistic documentation of the designer's creative sensibility and vision at a specific time and place. This collection is rooted in the dark, almost sinister atmosphere of the wild forest and haunted deteriorated cottages. In order to express this mystical mood, natural and durable outdoor fabrics were used in subdued organic, lightly washed colours. Comfortable loose layers, patterned knits, concealing hoods and utility backpacks recreate the authentic atmosphere of the area.

Sleeping bag and tent-like coats and jackets

Preliminary small figure sketches focusing on silhouette and proportion

*Fully-fashioned
fair isles, and
cut-and-sew knit
layering options*

DYLAN PAUL
MORAN TAVERNER

URBAN CHIC

Contemporary layers, minimalistic boxy shapes with occasional ties, strings and drapes are a practical and easy solution for modern sophisticated men. Concealed closures and simplicity of lines add to the incognito look. Black, navy, charcoal grey and shades of white, are urban colours resembling steel, concrete, cement and tinted glass.

CHINATI COAT

A reinterpretation of the classic trench coat, the CHINATI COAT features a double collar with a cross-body lapel, zipper front, back yoke, vented back, and snap-closure belt. Front storm flap conceals two chest pockets, for a total of four exterior pockets, and two interior pockets. Can attach to LINING COAT.

Double collar allows ties and sashes to be drawn through

CASE COAT

Features a free-hanging flap at the front that can be worn snapped closed, or draped around the neck as an innovative shawl.

Closes via front and shoulder snaps, as well as a belt that can be detached.

Two exterior side-seam pockets, two interior pockets.

Initial designs are sketched on tracing paper from the original figure templates, making it possible to focus on the silhouette and simple garment details. Once the series of looks is developed, the pencil sketches are scanned, outlined and rendered in Adobe Illustrator.

COAT SNAP, WHITE
metal and cotton, L30

COAT BUTTON
100 corozo, L40

UTILITY WAISTCOAT

Borrowed from the traditional waistcoat, this restyled garment strips the formality of the classic layering piece by omitting the back, and elongating the front to give room for truly accessible, on-seam welt pockets. Thus, the secondary layer adopts a function. Notch lapel with actual collar.

100% lightweight wool with 100% cotton voile lining.

Without a back or shoulders, the UTILITY WAIST-COAT fits only as its wearer wishes via adjustable back sashes, and is a truly universal and unisex style.

The realized garment folds and ties compactly on itself, making it a practical and packable layering piece.

This early fall collection includes pure wool and organic cotton duster coats, light trenches, easy jackets and cigarette pants.

The garments are both chic and comfortable, with adjustable straps and closures allowing changes in appearance and numerous unisex possibilities.

TUYEN TRAN

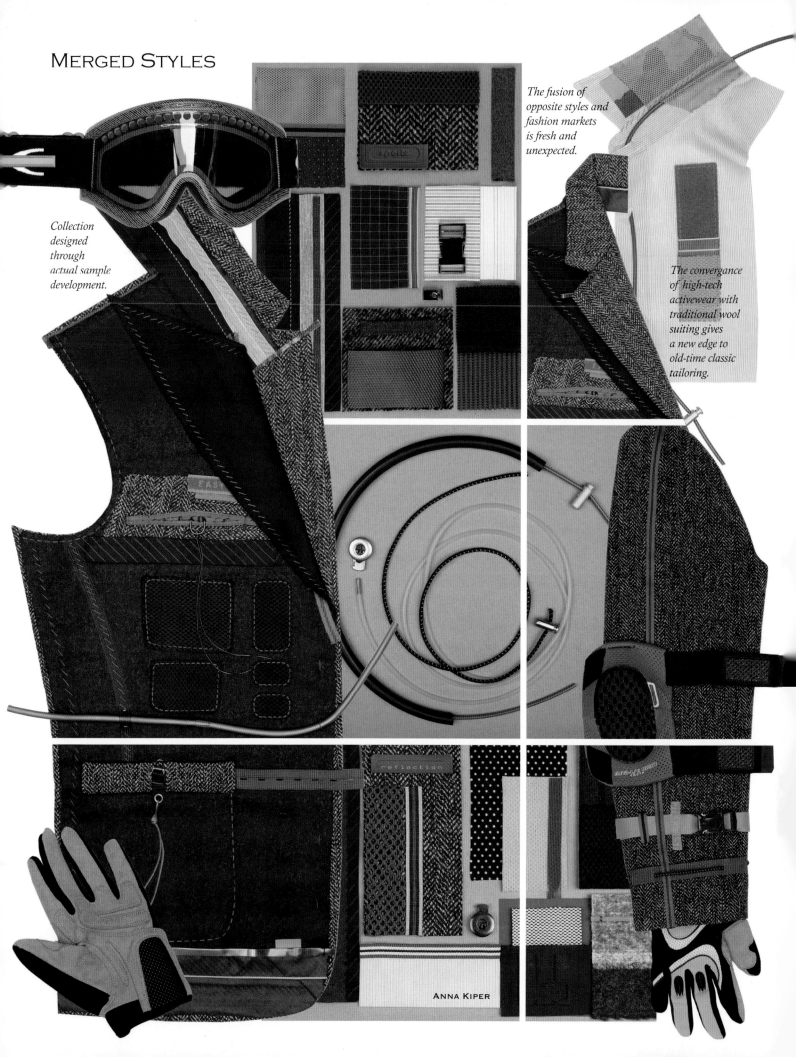

MERGED STYLES

Collection designed through actual sample development.

The fusion of opposite styles and fashion markets is fresh and unexpected.

The convergance of high-tech activewear with traditional wool suiting gives a new edge to old-time classic tailoring.

ANNA KIPER

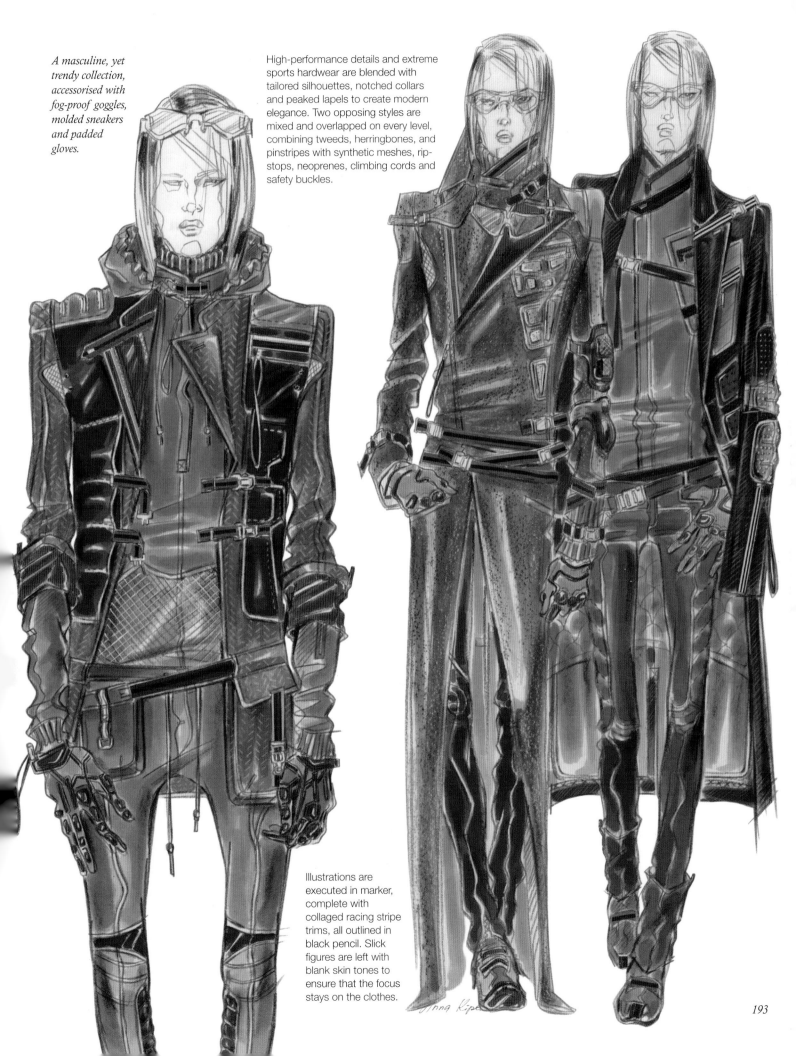

A masculine, yet trendy collection, accessorised with fog-proof goggles, molded sneakers and padded gloves.

High-performance details and extreme sports hardwear are blended with tailored silhouettes, notched collars and peaked lapels to create modern elegance. Two opposing styles are mixed and overlapped on every level, combining tweeds, herringbones, and pinstripes with synthetic meshes, rip-stops, neoprenes, climbing cords and safety buckles.

Illustrations are executed in marker, complete with collaged racing stripe trims, all outlined in black pencil. Slick figures are left with blank skin tones to ensure that the focus stays on the clothes.

trapunto top-stitching

built-in belts immitating obi sash

paper-bag waist

kimono v-neck

wrap and tie knits

A series of modern looks was created by playing with classic Japanese silk prints and jacquards, and analysing the kimono silhouette. Initial designs emerged in a series of freehand floats, which is a common way for designers to express their ideas without the restrictions of templates and croquis.

ANNA KIPER

Final figures are simple and static, executed in markers and collage.

CULTURAL INFLUENCES

Unexpected and contradicting inspiration is exciting and challenging, often resulting in the most unpredictable design outcomes. A traditional Japanese geisha outfit defines femininity and beauty – complete with the kimono, obi, white face paint and mesh headband. The traditional costume has been translated into an edgy menswear collection.

Floating red accents and nostalgic 80s-styled, sharp profiles give a specific rhythm to the presentation.

There are many various design approaches and work styles. Some designers start with art or historical research, some endlessly manipulate textiles, and others begin with vintage samples.

ANNA KIPER

MEN'S COUTURE

This flamboyant men's couture collection was conceived during a model drawing session. Working with a live model stimulates the imagination and helps capture the sensuality and movement of the clothes. The traditional design routine has been reversed. Typically inspiration research is the initial step. In this case, the illustration became the source of inspiration and generated the entire creative design process.

Design development can begin with a sketch, or even emerge from a sophisticated illustration.

Quick, freehand model studies become expressive design thumbnails helping to envision the customer and set the collection's mood.

Dramatic mood and theatrical styling of the model creates a vibrant vision of a spanish dancer.

To express the model's attitude, dynamic pencil lines were combined with red brush pen accents.

Anna Kiper

This collection is pushing the boundaries of traditional menswear into a new direction where corsets and skirts are acceptable. Classic bespoke shirts, vests, tuxedo trousers, cummerbunds and cravats are unexpectedly accented by harnesses, holster straps, corset belts and bandages.

ANNA KIPER

198

*vintage gangster-style
shirt with suspenders*

*motorcycle
laced-up jacket*

Intricate technical drawings
executed in ink pen combine
contrasting feminine and
masculine details, underlining
the obvious ambiguity of the
collection.

*high-waisted
tuxedo trouser*

holster tank

bridle-strapped corset

The passionate, electrifying atmosphere of the 'male tango' is captured in the contrasting colour story of black, white and shades of red. Next to traditional masculine pinstripes, sequins, beads, tulle and lace – all commonly associated with femininity – suddenly become very relevant.

Laced-up, strapped and corseted, the timeless menswear classics are transformed into haute couture chic.

ANNA KIPER

corseted coat

saddle-shoulder
leather harness

jodhpur
style
sleeves

garter belt vest

fan-lacing
bespoke shirt

stirrup breeches

CHILDRENSWEAR

The days where children are seen and not heard are long over, and savvy, young costumers are demanding a modern, comfortable wardrobes to accommodate their active lifestyles. However, for many centuries children's garments represented a shrunken version of adult clothing, closely imitating construction and fabric choice. Children's clothes were formal and restricting in fit, requiring children to behave maturely. Prior to the 20th century, children's clothing was mainly handcrafted at home, often recycled from adult garments.

After WWI, industrial commercial production of childrenswear began with the implementation of assembly lines, standardised sizing and the invention of modern fastenings like zippers, velcros and snaps. Traditional natural fibre fabrics like cotton knit, terry, twill, corduroy and denim remained popular for decades, however innovative man-made fabrics like nylon, lycra and synthetic fleece made children's clothing even more practical and durable.

In the 60s and 70s, children's designer labels and brands like Izod started to emerge. Recently some brands have been collaborating with famous men's and women's wear designers in a search of a fresh, creative point of view, free of childrenswear stereotypes.

Realistic illustrations

Realistic children's illustrations are commonly used in the fashion industry so that the proportions closely resemble actual children, and fashion garments can be presented in a more literal way. Stylised illustrations that have exaggerated proportions and 'cartoony' facial expressions, convey a distinct personality and are often appealing for childrenswear designers. Drawings could have oversized heads, inverted feet and mischievous attitudes.

Stylised illustrations

Categories:	*Markets:*	*Popular Brands:*
Infants	*Sportswear*	*Oililys*
Toddlers	*Outerwear*	*Zulily*
Children	*Dresses*	*Simonetta*
Tweens	*Sleepwear*	*Gap Kids*
Teens		*Crewcuts*
	Price Points:	*Diesel Kids*
	Budget	*Pale Cloud*
	Moderate	*Bonnie Young*
	Better	*Hannah Anderson*
	Designer	*Scotch and Soda Kids*

ANNA KIPER

202

Basic design principles apply to childrenswear. This Pre-fall collection of casual clothing and everyday activewear for boys, ages eight to fourteen, is inspired by the street sensibilities of New York skateboarding culture.

Mix-and-match aesthetic, textured solids with plaids and stripes in a series of layered looks suggest it was casually thrown together.

The use of a complimentary set of cargo shorts, hoodies and vests unites variations in silhouette and pattern with a colour palette of rustic heathers. This is street style with a sense of humor – preppy with an edge.

DIANA WOODSIDE

3D craft paper figures with removable paper and vinyl clothes

DIANA CHENG

CHILDREN'S ILLUSTRATION STYLES

Bright, fun and playful childrenswear sketches have no particular guidelines or standards. Stylised or realistic children's illustrations should be bold, full of character and clearly express the adorable and naïve nature of children. Fabric and paper collages, paintings on craft or coloured paper, and other unconventional media adds some sweet charm and personality to the sketch. Inspired by interactive childrenswear books and board games, 3D paper doll figures with removable clothes add an exciting element of surprise to a childrenswear presentation.

Mixed media

NEHA BHATIA

Markers and coloured pencils

IVY YESEUL KIM

*Marker with
pen outline*

JENNIFER LEE

*Gouache and
fabric collage on
coloured paper*

SCARLET JANG

*Watercolour with
digital enhancement*

EVELYN TAO

*Markers and
coloured pencils*

ALYSSA BUISHAS

This casual childrenswear collection was inspired by the Korean artist So Young Choi, who uses vintage, indigo cotton collages to create sceneries of villages and landscapes.

Illustrations in gouache and markers with yarn and fabric collages.

Textured surface created through fabric layering became an essential design approach for this denim-based collection. Focus was placed on various shades of blue and bright colour accents.

Textile samples created through patchwork, weaving, knitting, fabric dyeing and bleaching.

SEUL LEE

GRUNGE KIDS

This fantasy childrenswear story revolves around the narrative of a child living in a world without her parents. The child must fend for, and dress herself, resulting in unconventional ways of wearing necessary basics.

Wearing garments layered, backwards or inside-out, shoes that are seemingly 'broken,' and socks that are mismatched. The child's spirit and style was also designed with Grunge culture, and the poverty-stricken children in Helen Levitt's photography, in mind.

The collection feels spontaneous, and 'thrown together,' inviting endless possibilities for outfits.

HELEN CHEN

NATURE AND FASHION

The colourful and vibrant patterns of South America's native poisonous dart frog provide the inspiration for this collection of athletic wear for young girls. The designs incorporate a variety of sleek layered looks, cut and wrapped to create patterns that flow around the figure, yielding a variety of silhouettes in a spirit of youthful improvisation. The colour story for this line is drawn from the natural palette of the dart frogs themselves, with a variety of fabric treatment techniques employed to suggest the abstract and fractal beauty of Mother Nature, including ink dyes encased in fused plastic, wild patterns and chunky weaves.

These clothes are for girls taking their first steps out into the limelight, asserting their identities with clothing that is worn to be noticed, but without a hint of formality or adult sophistication.

DIANA WOODSIDE

KNITWEAR FOR TEENS

Quilted denims, corduroys and nylons are patchworked with chunky knits, creating playful and eccentric styles. Argyle patterns, ribs, intarsia and interlock stitches are all mixed together in a colourful collage of textures.

This knitwear-focused unisex collection intends to be sized from children to adults. It is inspired by the androgynous and quirky nature of London fashion, juxtaposing vintage looks with futurism, and the nostalgia of growing up in the 90s. Classic British style is seen in the fair isle knit patterns, while silhouettes mimic the feeling of growing into/out of clothes, hand-me-downs, snowsuits, layering and mismatching.

GIULIANA RAGGIANI

'refuse to grow-up' layers

twisted, variegated, yarns

ACCESSORIES

High-tech sneakers, designed with great attention to detail, are an object of desire for the urban athlete. They work as a fabulous highlight for these nostalgic outfits composed of a mid-century varsity jacket, jersey, basketball shorts and a terry cloth headband.

Accessories are always the finishing touch for any design collection. No fashion look is complete without appropriate footwear or a bag.

Sketches and diagrams of sneakers digitally executed.

Metal Zipper

elastic band

Patent Leather

Mesh

Patent Leather

Plastic square

Patent Leather

Rubber Sole

Eleastic Band

Mesh

Patent Leather

Patent Leather

elastic band

mesh

Patent Leather

Rubber Sole

rubber sole

Plastic sole

ICK JEONG AHN

Serving as the 'last styling touch,' accessories are expected to be functional by the average consumer. Coordinated with the customer's attitude and style, accessories should complement the clothes either blending with the outfit or becoming an accent and focal point of the look.

MAGGIE TOOKMANIAN

Steel-cage boots, a braided leather visor or heat-molded plastic bag with a hand-casted metal frame are conceptual and almost surreal fashion objects. Experimental accessories are not always practical, but can be show-stoppers and a great touch for a minimalistic outfit.

213

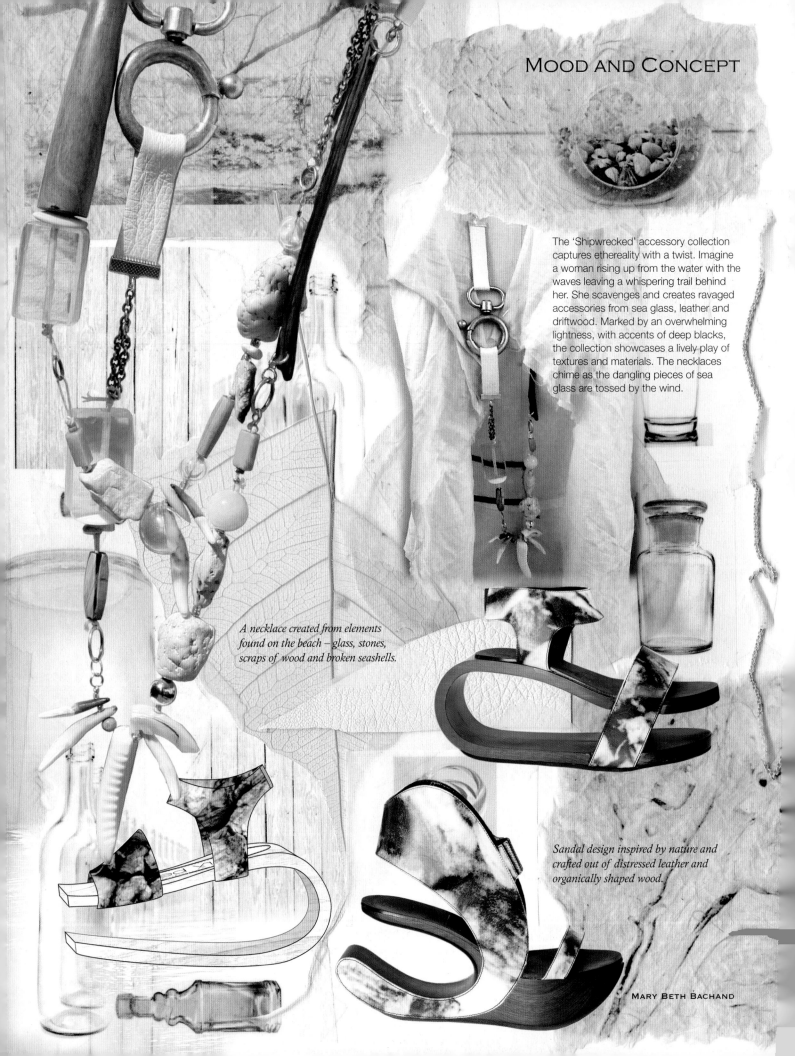

MOOD AND CONCEPT

The 'Shipwrecked' accessory collection captures ethereality with a twist. Imagine a woman rising up from the water with the waves leaving a whispering trail behind her. She scavenges and creates ravaged accessories from sea glass, leather and driftwood. Marked by an overwhelming lightness, with accents of deep blacks, the collection showcases a lively play of textures and materials. The necklaces chime as the dangling pieces of sea glass are tossed by the wind.

A necklace created from elements found on the beach – glass, stones, scraps of wood and broken seashells.

Sandal design inspired by nature and crafted out of distressed leather and organically shaped wood.

MARY BETH BACHAND

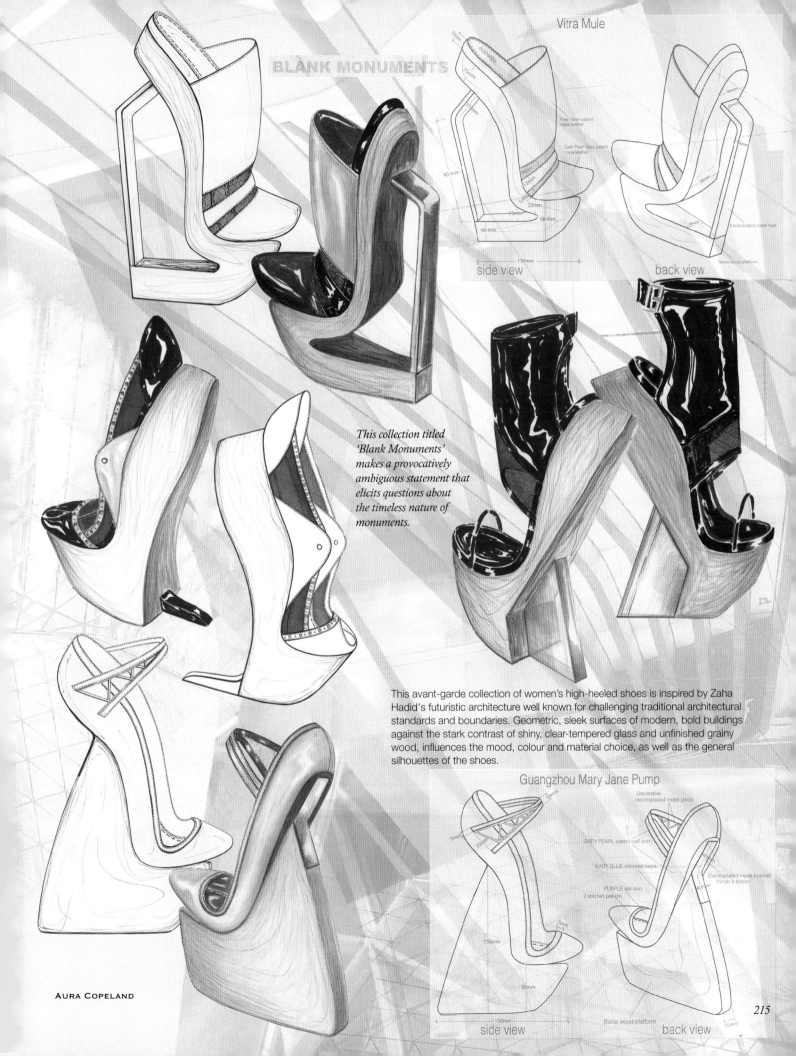

Vitra Mule

Pearl Grey patent napa leather

Dark Pearl Grey patent napa leather

90 mm

25mm

15mm

68 mm

40 mm

130mm

side view

Electroplated metal heel

Balsa wood platform

back view

This collection titled 'Blank Monuments' makes a provocatively ambiguous statement that elicits questions about the timeless nature of monuments.

This avant-garde collection of women's high-heeled shoes is inspired by Zaha Hadid's futuristic architecture well known for challenging traditional architectural standards and boundaries. Geometric, sleek surfaces of modern, bold buildings against the stark contrast of shiny, clear-tempered glass and unfinished grainy wood, influences the mood, colour and material choice, as well as the general silhouettes of the shoes.

Guangzhou Mary Jane Pump

Decorative electroplated metal piece

GREY PEARL patent calf skin

BABY BLUE mirrored napa

Electroplated metal bracket 15mm X 80mm

PURPLE kid skin
2 stitches per cm

150mm

50mm

130mm

side view

Balsa wood platform

back view

AURA COPELAND

215

Pocket with Lenticular Print Pocket Entry

Lenticular Print with rollout

→ Lenticular Print seam into Leather lining

→ Center seam to ensure curvature

→ White glossy paint, achieve the porcelain look

Steps taken from concept to final product.

The holographic print is added for a futuristic twist to the classic silhouette of the iconic satchel bag. The flap is removable, giving the wearer an option to match their outfits.

8mm binding

22cm

10cm

9cm

CONCERIA STEFANIA STEFANIL

This accessories collection questions our preconceived way of seeing familiar things. The holographic print used in these designs is composed from a series of images collapsed into one flat surface. As a result, the print displays different patterns when viewed from different angles. When the shoes and bag are worn, the print changes and transforms with the movement of the wearer.

Painted White (Glossy)

1"
¾"

2"

1¾"

2"   1"   3"

extended heel = 1½

Digitally illustrated

*Illustrated with
watercolour*

*The holographic panels placed on
the heels and soles of the shoes
emphasise the geometric shapes.
Shoe samples are made from the
same mold, experimenting with
different colours and materials.*

*Suede, pony skin and lacquered
leather is used for the top of the
shoes, with sculpted-plastic soles
and heels.*

*The shoes are designed with the wearer in mind.
Square heels provide a great deal of support and the
centre of the structure is carved out to hug the foot
and allow for more comfort.*

YINGSHI JUNE LIN

217

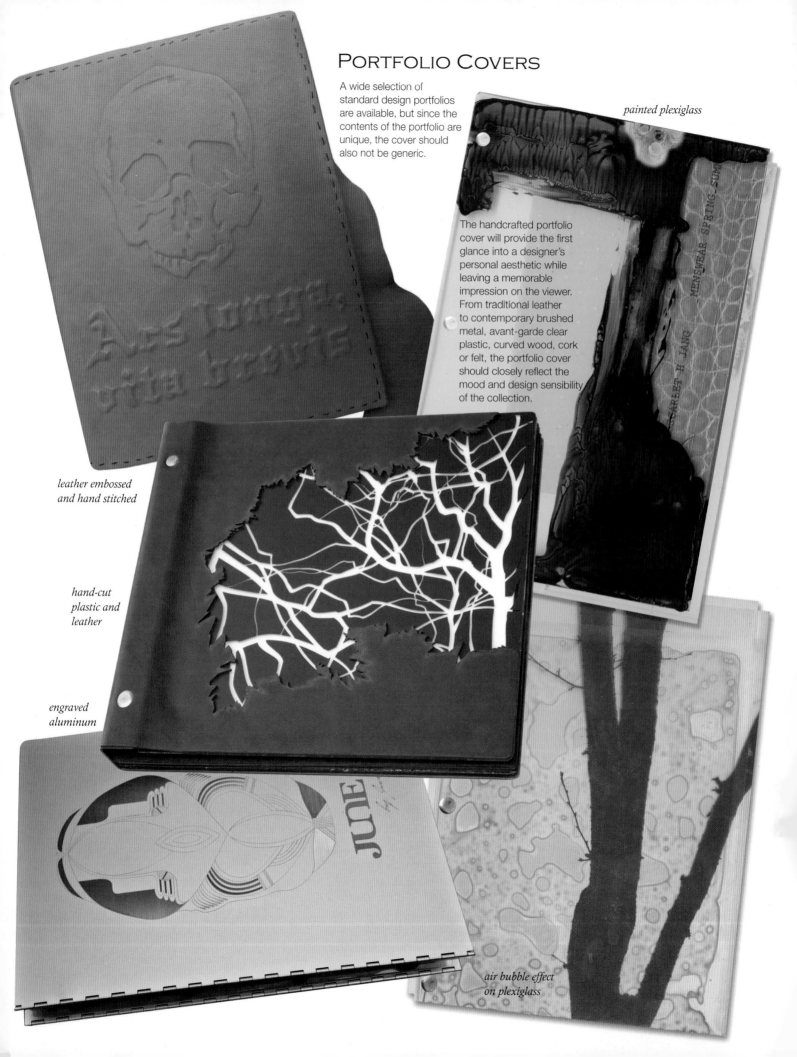

PORTFOLIO COVERS

A wide selection of standard design portfolios are available, but since the contents of the portfolio are unique, the cover should also not be generic.

painted plexiglass

The handcrafted portfolio cover will provide the first glance into a designer's personal aesthetic while leaving a memorable impression on the viewer. From traditional leather to contemporary brushed metal, avant-garde clear plastic, curved wood, cork or felt, the portfolio cover should closely reflect the mood and design sensibility of the collection.

leather embossed and hand stitched

hand-cut plastic and leather

engraved aluminum

air bubble effect on plexiglass

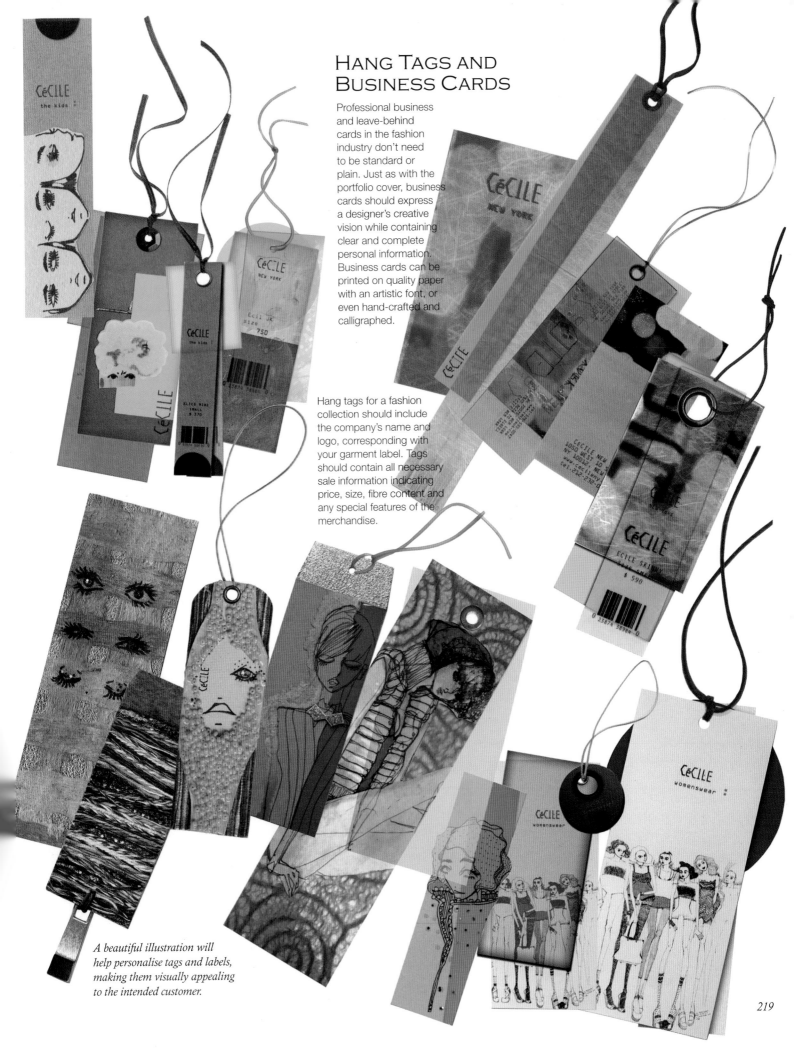

HANG TAGS AND BUSINESS CARDS

Professional business and leave-behind cards in the fashion industry don't need to be standard or plain. Just as with the portfolio cover, business cards should express a designer's creative vision while containing clear and complete personal information. Business cards can be printed on quality paper with an artistic font, or even hand-crafted and calligraphed.

Hang tags for a fashion collection should include the company's name and logo, corresponding with your garment label. Tags should contain all necessary sale information indicating price, size, fibre content and any special features of the merchandise.

A beautiful illustration will help personalise tags and labels, making them visually appealing to the intended customer.

THE LOOK BOOK

The photo look book, featuring finished garments and accessories, is a great addition to any design portfolio.

Beautifully styled, dynamic photographs taken in a setting with a model that reflects the aesthetic and unique vision of the collection, will illuminate and showcase the final outcome of the design process. When producing the look book, carefully chosen fonts and paper, as well as dramatic, artistically composed photographs, will accentuate the mood of the collection.

The 'Parachute' menswear collection is all about lightness, pure cotton layering and easy, playful styling. The absence of gravity is expressed through bright white, weightless fabrics, and functional loose garments with adjustable strings, cords and mesh inserts.

SEUNG YUN KIM

220

'Le Carceri d'Invenzione' means 'Imaginary Prisons' in Italian. The inspiration for this collection was the etchings of prisons created by Italian artist, Giovanni Battista Piranesi. His realistic visions of dark cavernous dungeons, draped with chains and ropes strongly convey desperation and loneliness.

The austere, black-and-white photographs, along with the dramatic look of the model, enhances the collection's mood.

A sense of entrapment was created through cocoon silhouettes with sculpted collars, spiral seams, straps and elastic bandages. Various black textiles were collaged in one garment, creating a deep monochromatic texture.

ELSA ELLIES

ACKNOWLEDGEMENTS

This book would not have been possible without the talented individuals who generously offered their advice, time, skills and resources. A special thanks to all of the design students at the Fashion Institute of Technology and Parsons New School for Design for contributing their original work, which makes this book a rich and valuable resource for future students and emerging designers.

A most special thanks to my husband, Rick Shifman, for his enormous help and contribution. Without his support, I would never have been able to complete this project. Thanks to my mom, Maria Kiper, who always believed in me, and to my sons, Daniel and Jordan, for their love and patience.

l = left; r = right; t = top; b = bottom; c = centre

Design Contributors

Ike Jeong Ahn 212
Anthony Argentina 28–9
Mary Beth Bachand 214
Claudia Baik 84–5
Olga Bely 27
Neha Bhatia 182, 204
Sarah Blanche Blondes 34
Carteris Travanti Brown 170 bl–171
Alyssa Buishas 205
Elizabeth Carol 73 c painting
Amy Yu Hsuan Chen 70–1
Helen Chen 76 cut felt, 207
Diana Cheng 30, 182, 204
Paula Cheng 140–5
Shany Cohen 78 felted samples
Aura Copeland 215
Devon Dagworthy 80 (1, 2, 3, 4, 6)
Guy Dempster 126
Peter Do 106–7
Doha 163–5
Elsa Ellies 42–5, 218 c, 221
Marisol Estelles Bilbao 178 tl, photo manipulation
Danielle Frankel 76 robes and lace, 172–3
Nicole Ghosn and Politecnico Calzaturiero 118–9 (shoes)
Domingo A. Gómez 76 vegetable dyes
Wenda Gu, calligraphy 23
Victoria Hayes 78 hand knit, stencil transfer, dip-dye, photo tl, 79
Jun Juyeon Hong 31, 52–3
Scarlet Hye Rim Jang 26, 28, 58–9, 72 colour testers, 75 frames, 81 (7–12), 160–1 leather samples, 184–5, 205, 218 tr, br ,219
Yoonhee Joe 100–1, 183
Elin Johansson 35, 99, 148–9
Min Kyung Jung 170 red dress
Soojin Kang 152–5
Michael Visay Khamphasong 77 clear tubes textile
Noriko Kikuchi 39, 50–1
Ivy Yeseul Kim 204
Sunghee Kim 128
Seung Yun Kim 220
Minji Koo 218 tl
Hooin Lee 16 bl
Jennifer Lee 205
Jin Hwa Lee 99, 183
Lisa Lee 99
Mariah Lee 81 (10, 11, 12) digital art
Seul Lee 206
Jiayu Li 98
Jie Li 62–3
Yingshi June Lin 56–7, 104–5, 126–7, 216–7, 218 bl
Judith Lopez 134–5 samples
Feitong Lu 28–9
Ou Ma 28, 46–9
Karen Mascarenhas 121 digital art, textiles
Jihye Min 183
Dylan Paul Moran Taverner 182–3, 188–9
Joshua Myrie 60–1
Maggie Norris Couture 20 hunting jacket, 22–3, 130, 165 bra
Jing Ying Ou 77 wire and beads textile
Jay Padia 109 antique jewelry
Adrienne Perlstein 186–7
Riet-D-Peters 77–8 heat-melted angelina fibre, fine plastic cords knitted with paillettes
Giuliana Raggiani 210–1
Jaylin Yongchu Rhew 98
Elspeth Schulze 167
Chris Hyehriyoung Shin 76, 78 screen-printed textiles
A Ram Sim 169

Joseph Singh 36–7
Renée Smith 157 figure illustrations
Yea Jin Song 78 felted yarns, digital print
Levi Steffensen 124
Albertus Swanepoel hats 23
Mary Symczak 66–7, 102–3
Evelyn Tao 205
Maggie Tookmanian 213
Tuyen Tran 190–1
Jessica Velez 76 stones and chains, 150–1
Maria Wang Zeying 24–5, 29 tr, 32–3, 75 tr
Brit Frady-Williams 16 street punk outfits
Mayumi Yamamoto 38, 174–7
Heewon Yang 98
Yvonne Zhou 77 folded and braided leather strips
Quinn Zhu 68–9, 146 rib, jacquard, 147

Anna Kiper front/back cover illustrations 2–4, 7–13, 18 br, 20–1, 22–3 silk painting, beading, embroidery layouts, illustrations, 30 flats, 40–1, 64–5, 74–5, 76–7 (patchwork, appliqué, fused tulle), 80–81 (5,13,14), 82–83, 86–97, 108–123, 125, 129, 130–9, 146, 147 figure illustrations, 156–7, 158–162, 163–5 flats, textiles, 168, 171 flats, textiles, 178–9, 181, 192–202, 224

All layouts are original and designed by Anna Kiper.

Text Contributors

Chloe Chapin with Anna Kiper 8–13
Janet Chung, editing
Elaine Press 37
David Wolfe 14–5, 17 bc

Photographers

Olivier Bacquet 122 bl red rails
Luke Baxter 19 bl, br
Jena Cumbo 35, 148–9
Joseph H. Dennis 122 tl subway redlines
Dave Frieder 52 Queensboro and Williamsburg bridges
Mariano Garcia 154 tl–155 t, br
Blair Getz Mezibov 43, 45
Yulia Gorbachenko 17 uptown chic, hip-hop 144–5
Yu Hou 84–5
Mark Kessell 82–3 Title: Dialog With Blindness; Title: Mere Opportunities V; Title: Mere Opportunities IV; Title: Analog Consciousness III
Damien Wook Hyun Kim 220
Jayoung Kim 17 eccentric style
Moon Chung Kim 16 futuristic emo
Anna Kiper 16 Japanese lolita,17 urban goth, 23 corset, 109, 113, 115, 130 model, 196 model
Kara Kochalko 210–1
Shinhwa Koo 170 l
Anna Moller 50
Timu Mori 17 anime style
Phillip Ng Knightmare6 16 street punk
Dylan Reyes 213
Morgan Salyer (assistant photographer) 20 c, 22–3, 131 necklace, 136 tc, c

Jennifer Santanastaso 169
Anatoly Shifman textiles/props 21, 30, 40, 64–5, 72–5, 76 bl, 78 t–9 r, 88 l, 101 b, 108 t, 112 tr, 114, 116–7, 120 tl, 122 br, 130 tl, 146, 156, 158, 162–3, 164–5, 170 cr, 192, 194–5, 196 c, 198 tl
Rick Shifman textiles/props 4, 14 l, 18–9, 41, 44 , 73 tc, 76–7, 108 b, 112 br, 116 b,118–9, 121 br, 129, 132 bc, 134–5, 147, 150–1l, 160, 165 c, 178, 181, 190 tl, 202, 218 tl c
Zev Starr-Tambor 36–7
David Surowiecki 57 t, 216–7
Kedrick Walker 16 rap glamour
Yanique Wilson 19 tl, tr, 20 c, 22–3, 80 original image, 131 necklace, 136 tc, c
Art Wolfe 65, Getty Images ®, Title: Kenya, Masai tribesperson, close-up of face with head-dress

Models / Model Agencies

Nejilka Arias 19 tr, tl
Michelle Bobe 211
Jolynn Carpenter 2
Tong Cheng 16 Japanese lolita
Claire Geist 166
Arthur John Gonzales 210–1
Alexdra Grady with Muse (agency) 50, 154–5
Alika Hall 17 urban goth
Joshua B. Homic 17 eccentric style
Identities Model Inc. (agency) 57
Erica Michele Jamrog 75 c, 80–1
Tereza Janakova 57 r, l, 36–7, 213
Collete Laporta 22–3, 136
Hooin Lee 16 futuristic emo
Fay Leshner 130,113
Jessa Doll (Jessica Pahlck) 16 street punk
Robert Thomas Warden (agency) 220
Sade with Fenton Moon (agency) 17 uptown chic, hip-hop
Andrew Shields 17 urban goth
Kristina Velkova 35, 148–9
Ignacio Villeta 196
Alexa Nicole Whipple 16 street punk
Shyloh Wilkinson 57 c
Stephon E. Williams 16 rap glamour, 17 eccentric style
Judy C. Yang 169

Stylists/Hair/Makeup Artists

Amira Alkaysi 17 uptown chic, hip-hop
Marika Aoki 22–3
Kathe Cameron 16 street punk
Christopher Campbell 43, 45, 221
Davis Carrasquillo 17, uptown chic, hip-hop
Janet Chung 80 original image styling
Sophie Ono 50, 57
Jessa Doll (Jessica Pahlck) 16 street punk
Cenita Scott
17 uptown chic, hip-hop
Shingo Shibata 17 uptown chic, hip-hop
Mari Shten 17 uptown chic, hip-hop
Takayoshi Tsukisawa 220
Pia Vivas 35, 148–9
Martial Vivot of Salon pour Hommes 43, 45, 221
Judy C. Yang 169

Special Contributors and Picture Credits

Olga Borodulina, research assistant
Felicia Da Costa, consultant
Ellen Sideri ESP Trend Forecast 14–5, 180
Christine Foden, d.cipher fm Trend Forecast 14–5, 180
Getty Images 65 tl
GoRunway 18 Donna Karen Autumn/Winter 2012/13,
    54–5 Calvin Klein Spring/Summer 2009,
    Alexander McQueen Autumn/Winter 2008/9,
Comme des Garçon Spring/Summer 2008,
    Michael Kors Autumn/Winter 2012/13
Ernst Haeckel, *Art Forms in Nature* by Haeckel by
    Dover Publications, 167
Scarlet Hye Rim Jang, research assistant
Valeriya Miller, graphic design

*I would also like to thank Valeriya Miller,
Janet Chung, Maggie Norris, David Wolfe,
Ellen Sideri, Chloe Chapin, Yanique Wilson,
Anatoly Shifman, Scarlet Hye Rim Jang and
Olga Borodulina. Without your time and
dedication, this book would not be as beautiful
and complete as it is.*

*To anyone who has been left out in error, my sincerest
apologies and thank you.*

RESOURCES

Museums and Costume Galleries

United States

The Metropolitan Museum of Art
The Costume Institute
www.metmuseum.org

The Museum at FIT
www.fitnyc.edu/museum

The Brooklyn Museum
www.brooklynmuseum.org

Smithsonian Cooper-Hewitt
National Design Museum in New York
www.cooperhewitt.org

Los Angeles County Museum of Art | LACMA
www.lacma.org

United Kingdom

Fashion Museum
www.museumofcostume.co.uk

Victoria and Albert Museum
www.vam.ac.uk

Italy

Galeria del Costume
http://www.uffizi.firenze.it/musei/?m=costume

Museum Salvatore Ferragamo
http://www.museoferragamo.it

France

Museé de la Mode et du Costume
http://palaisgalliera.paris.fr

Museé Des Arts de la Mode
http://www.lesartsdecoratifs.fr

Fashion Libraries

New York Public Library
Mid-Manhattan Library
www.nypl.org/locations/mid-manhattan-library

Berg Fashion Library
http://www.bergfashionlibrary.com

Fashion Institute of Technology Library, New York
www.fitnyc.edu/library.asp

London College of Fashion Library
www.bergfashionlibrary.com

Albright Fashion Library
http://www.albrightnyc.com

Fashion Schools

United States

Fashion Institute of Technology
www.fitnyc.edu

Parsons The New School for Design
www.newschool.edu/parsons

Pratt Institute
www.pratt.edu

Savannah State University
www.savannahstate.edu

Otis College of Art and Design
www.otis.edu

United Kingdom

Central Saint Martins
University of Arts London
www.arts.ac.uk/csm

London College of Fashion
University of Arts London
www.arts.ac.uk/fashion

Kingston University London
www.kingston.ac.uk

Royal College of Art
www.rca.ac.uk

Italy

Academia di Costume e di Moda
www.accademiacostumeemoda.it

Istituto Marangoni
www.istitutomarangoni.com

Polimoda
www.polimoda.com

France

Ecole Duperre
www.essa-duperre.scola.ac-paris.fr

ESMOD
www.esmod .com

Studio Bercot
www. studio-berçot.com

Fabrics and Trims

United States

B&J Fabrics
www.bandjfabrics.com

Mood Fabrics
www.moodfabrics.com

New York Elegant Fabrics
www.nyelegantfabrics.com

Pacific Trimming
www.pacifictrimming.com

M&J trimming
www.mjtrim.com

Global Leathers
www.globalleathers.com

Leather Impact
www.leatherimpact.com

Steinlauf & Stoller (sewing supply)
www.steinlaufandstoler.com

United Kingdom

Borovick Fabrics
www.borovickfabricsltd.co.uk

Cloth House
www.clothhouse.com

Barnett Lawson Trimmings
www.broadwicksilks.com

Kleins
www.kleins.co.uk

Trends/Colour Forecasting

Trend Union
Edelkoort Inc.
www.edelkoort.com/

Promostyl
www.promostyl.com

The Doneger Group
www.doneger.com

Color Portfolio
www.colorportfolio.com

PANTONE Color
www.pantone.com

The Cotton Incorporated
www.cottoninc.com

ESP Trendlab
www.esptrendlab.com

Peclers Paris
www.peclersparis.com

d.cipher fm
dcipherfm.com

Style.com
www.style.com

WGSN Trend Forecasting
www.wgsn.com

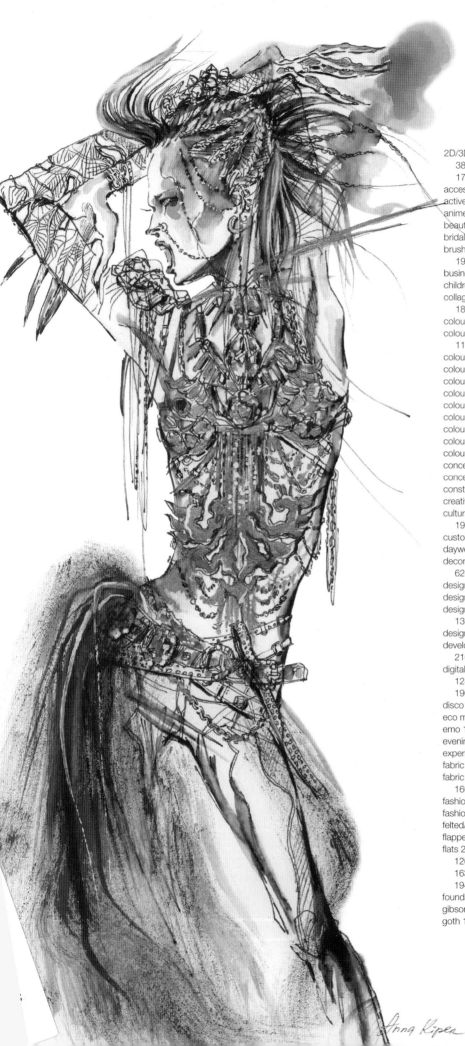

INDEX

Anna Kiper